Gifts from the Heart

10 Communication Skills for
Developing More Loving Relationships

RANDY FUJISHIN

West Valley College
Saratoga, California

ACADA BOOKS
San Francisco

D1416598

ACADA BOOKS
1850 Union Street Suite 1216
San Francisco, California 94123
Telephone: (415) 776–2325
E-mail: acada@ix.netcom.com

Copyeditor: David Sweet
Proofreader: Helen Walden
Indexer: Patricia Deminna
Interior Designer: Shelley Firth
Cover Designer: Dunn + Associates
Back Cover Writer: Susan Kendrick
Compositor: Pale Moon Productions

Publisher's Cataloging-in-Publication
(Provided by Quality Books, Inc.)

Fujishin, Randy.
Gifts from the heart : ten communication skills for developing
more loving relationships / Randy Fujishin — 1st ed.
p. cm.
Includes bibliographical references and index.
ISBN: 0-9655029-2-9

1. Interpersonal communication.   I. Title.

BF637.C45F85 1997   153.6
QBI97-41309

Printed in the United States of America
1   2   3   4   5 — 02   01   00   99   98

For Vicky,
Tyler, and Jared

Also by Randy Fujishin

Discovering the Leader Within

The Natural Speaker

Contents

❦

v
~

Preface

Deep in our hearts we all desire relationships that are loving, healthy, and meaningful. We want relationships that nurture our spirit, encourage our growth, and even make us laugh in the quiet of the night. We yearn for this. Yet many times, this is not our experience.

- Kathy has been dating Paul for seven months. They seem to enjoy each other's company, but she's frustrated with his inability or unwillingness to share his feelings. Kathy wishes she could tell Paul about her frustration or get him to open up, but she doesn't know how.

- Joanne had been best friends with Marcy since their college days fifteen years ago. They were like sisters, but six months ago they had an argument and haven't spoken since. Joanne would like to break the ice and talk about what happened, but she feels Marcy should call first. Joanne wishes to soften, to forgive, but she doesn't know how.

- Tim, a single, thirty-two-year-old man, receives a letter from his mother saying that she's coming to visit for three days. Tim is immediately paralyzed with dread, knowing how his controlling mother will drive him crazy. Tim wants to be kinder and more loving to his mom, and communicate his boundaries, but he doesn't know how.

Do any of these situations sound familiar to you? Perhaps it's not an issue of disclosing feelings, communicating forgiveness, or stating boundaries. Maybe you don't know how to listen effectively, communicate acceptance, or ask questions. Or perhaps you have difficulty complimenting, resolving conflict, or encouraging growth in others.

Because no one is born with the communication skills that bring us closer to those we love, they must be learned. As a relationship communications instructor for twenty-four years and a marriage and family therapist for ten years, I have had the privilege of helping men and women, just like you, learn, practice, and improve ten fundamental communication skills necessary for any long-term relationship. I encourage my students and clients to view each skill as a gift they can share rather than simply a behavior they can implement. This perspective empowers them to participate more fully in their relationships by giving these gifts of communication instead of waiting to receive what the other person might offer. These gifts, whether intended for a romantic partner, family member, or friend, can greatly enhance and strengthen any relationship you want to improve.

The communication gifts and concepts presented in this book do not represent any one particular theoretical orientation or belief. Instead, they reflect a broad range of skills and ideas collected during my years as a teacher and counselor. My experiences as husband and father have also greatly influenced and guided my journey to become a giver of gifts.

It is my hope that you will read this book with an open mind, a willingness to try new things, and a desire to change. It is also my wish that you will become a giver of gifts. Gifts that will empower you to connect with those you love. Gifts that will ultimately enable you to experience relationships that will nurture your spirit, encourage your growth, and even make you laugh in the quiet of the night. Gifts from the heart.

Acknowledgments

Many people have contributed to the creation of this book. My deepest appreciation goes to Robin Geller Romer, my editor, for her expert guidance and gentle sense of balance, and to Brian Romer, publisher of Acada Books, for his wisdom, boundless enthusiasm, and friendship. May you enjoy your island retreat in the years ahead.

To Ralph Banks, San Jose State University; Claire Calcagno, DeAnza College; Dr. Robert Christenson, California Polytechnic State University; Donald E. Jones, University of Texas—Austin; Dr. Carol Raupp, California State University—Bakersfield; Dr. W. Fred Stultz, California Polytechnic at San Luis Obisbo; and Mary Waldner, Marriage, Family, and Child Counselor, for reading the original manuscript and offering such valuable feedback and suggestions.

To my mother and father, for giving me the gift of love. And to Paul Sanders for being my brother in this lifetime.

My deepest love to our sons, Jared and Tyler, for being joyous gifts of happiness and wonder. And finally, to my wife, Vicky, my most precious gift of all.

Relationships Require Giving

> "You cannot love without giving."
> —Mother Teresa

There are sacred places we carry in our hearts forever. They become a part of our interior landscape, rich reminders of who we are and what we're about. And just as surely as they etch their memories of time and place upon our souls, we leave the echoes of our whispers within their borders. I carry such a place in my heart.

The beach was small and secluded, located at the end of a dirt road somewhere south of Kona, Hawaii. From its half-moon shore, the sea and the sky seemed to reach out to the horizon in soft blues and emerald greens. My wife and I sat on the warm sand, feeling the magic of this beach for the first time. It was the second day of our honeymoon, and we would return often to this place in the years to follow.

On that day, I noticed a couple at the other end of the beach who arrived in the early afternoon. I watched them in the distance as they held hands, talked in whispers, and seemed to enjoy each other's company. Before they left, they strolled over and said hello to us. To my surprise, they were much older than I had thought—both were in their seventies.

As they talked with us, we learned they had been married for over fifty years and had raised four children. I asked the husband for his secret to such a long-lasting relationship. Without hesitation he replied, "I learned to be a giver and not a taker."

"You see," said Henry, "when we were first married, I thought Alice would provide a good home for me—she would give me companionship and love. Plus, she was the best-looking woman in Kilua-Kona. All I could think about was what Alice could give me."

"Well, after fifty years of marriage," he concluded, "I've learned to be a giver and not a taker."

To be a giver and not a taker. Those words have followed me since that afternoon on the half-moon beach many years ago. I believe that this shift from self to other—from receiver to giver—is the fundamental attitude we need to adopt in order to develop, nurture, and improve our relationships with those people we love, whether a romantic partner, family member, or friend. All loving relationships require giving.

An individual can give countless gifts, both large and small, to another person in a lifetime. Entire industries are based on this fact. We spend billions of dollars each year on gifts for our loved ones, hoping to please and satisfy them. Yet how quickly the newness of our gifts fade and the inadequacies and frustrations of our relationships resurface. Sooner or later we realize the most significant gifts we can give are found not in shops, but in our hearts. These are the gifts of love. No loving relationship can exist without gifts such as communicating for connection, accepting others, listening for understanding, asking questions, enlarging others, flowing with conflict, showing you care, and forgiving. These gifts help you develop any connection into a more lasting, loving relationship.

But what is a relationship? In order to answer this question, we'll explore the three levels of relationships, the three stages of relationship development, and five principles of healthy relationships.

LEVELS OF RELATIONSHIPS

Not all relationships are the same. They vary in depth, duration, and function. Marianne Williamson, author of *Return to Love*, suggests three levels of relationships, which I find helpful in understanding our connections with other people. The three levels are the casual encounter, the sustained relationship, and the lifelong relationship.

The Casual Encounter

The first level of relationships is the casual encounter. Saying hello to a stranger on the street, smiling at someone in an elevator, and exchanging pleasantries with a bank teller are examples of the casual encounter. There is no real depth or commitment at this level of relationships. But our casual encounters let us practice our interpersonal communication skills. They help us improve our public personalities. Whatever weaknesses we have at this level are magnified at the other two levels. If we're grouchy here, it will be more difficult to be loving with people at the other two levels.

The Sustained Relationship

In the second level, two people are in a fairly intense relationship for a period of time (three to sixty months) and then terminate the relationship for a variety of reasons. The individuals can be coworkers, neighbors, friends, lovers, even husband and wife, but eventually the relationship ends and the two go their separate ways. The experiences and learning that both encounter at the sustained relationship can be significantly important and leave a lasting imprint on their minds and souls.

The Lifelong Relationship

Lifelong relationships are relatively few during our journey on this earth. But from them we learn our most valuable lessons. The people with whom we are in lifetime relationships are not necessarily those we like or enjoy. They are in our lives to teach us our most important lessons—to forgive, to endure, to show us our limits, and to love. Often these individuals provide us with a lifetime of love, joy, and peace. Yet even lifelong relationships come at a price. And that price is to learn how to accept other human beings—their shortcomings and weaknesses, as well as their strengths.

Just as there are different levels of relationships, there are also different stages of development within each level, especially in sustained and lifelong relationships. Let's look at these three stages of development.

STAGES OF RELATIONSHIP DEVELOPMENT

Ruth, one of my dearest friends, has been married for more than fifty-five years. I once asked her to what she attributed her long marriage to Bob. She smiled and calmly said, "The knowledge that some decades are harder than others." Some *decades* are harder than others! Decades! I had never heard marriage or relationship put in those terms.

Each level of relationship goes through changes or stages of development. There are numerous models of relationship development. Some are complex, resembling a flowchart for a multilevel corporation, and others are much simpler in design. For our purposes, I have chosen the simplest model I know—sparkle, conflict, and resolution. Just about every relationship model includes some variation of these three stages.

Stage 1: Sparkle

The sparkle stage is when the relationship begins and everything is going well. This includes the euphoria of a first romance, the optimism of a new friendship, or the long-sought arrival of a first child. Everything sparkles with newness, freshness, and possibility. Time seems to fly. Each meeting is anticipated with longing and excitement, and nothing seems to go wrong. Little or no conflict exists in the relationship. Everyone puts a best foot forward, and things couldn't be better.

Stage 2: Conflict

The inevitable conflict stage is when differences of opinions, feelings, wants, or behaviors surface in the relationship. This is a critical stage because the way people confront or deal with conflict will determine the quality of the relationship. The conflict stage is not a bad thing, but rather it can be an invitation to a deeper, more authentic relationship. Conflict in the relationship indicates that the individuals are beginning to assert their individuality, their truer selves. How they deal with conflict will determine the quality of the relationship. Many individuals abandon relationships at this stage, opting for the eternal sparkle of one shallow relationship after another, never really investing in the more costly requirements deeper relationships demand.

Stage 3: Resolution

The resolution stage represents the outcome or solution to the conflict the individuals have reached. If conflict is cooperatively addressed, there is a good chance the individuals will discover common ground, solutions will emerge, and the relationship will grow. Not all conflicts can be resolved and those that can't often lead to the termination of the relationship. But those conflicts that are successfully managed and negotiated are the source of greater relationship strength and satisfaction. All relationships require the successful negotiation of conflict to remain vital and healthy.

The Circular Nature of the Relationship Model

No relationship will follow these three stages exactly as described. Some relationships will emphasize one stage over another while other relationships might begin with conflict and move to the sparkle stage. In other words, this relationship model has a circular nature. Unlike a linear model, which moves from Stage 1 to 2 to 3 in a straight line and then ends, this model returns to its beginning, time and time again. After one conflict has been resolved, we can return to the sparkle stage of a relationship, experience new conflicts, resolve them, and once again return to the sparkle stage. The challenge is in bringing new forms of sparkle to the relationship, while creatively and cooperatively solving one thing after another during the journey together. Here are five relationship principles to keep in mind as you face this challenge.

PRINCIPLES OF HEALTHY RELATIONSHIPS

No one approach or prescription guarantees a successful, satisfying relationship with another person. Whether the relationship is with a romantic partner, family member, or friend, the territory is always unique and each journey is new. No map exists that charts every curve, hill, and valley of a relationship. Yet over the years I have observed and experienced some general principles of healthy relationships.

Relationships Are Not Perfect

One of the most common myths about relationships is that everything must be perfect for the relationship to be good. Like in the movies, we want our relationships to be free of conflict and filled with love and passion. Yet most good relationships are far from perfect. Irritations, shortcomings, failures, and disappointments always crop up.

Although no relationship is perfect, I believe that 80 percent of a healthy relationship is working at any given time and only 20 percent of the relationship is not. I call this my **80/20 rule**. The trouble is that we tend to focus our attention on the 20 percent that's not working and ignore all the wonderful aspects of a relationship that are working. We sabotage the relationship by choosing to focus on the negative. A healthier choice is to concentrate more of our attention on the 80 percent. Rather than focus on your loved one's snoring, leaving off the toothpaste cap, or an occasional criticism, try to identify, compliment, and reward your loved one's loyalty, encouragement, financial responsibility, commitment, and other areas of the relationship that are working.

Relationships Do Not Give You Everything

No relationship will provide you with everything you need to be happy. There isn't one single relationship that can satisfy all your needs, desires, and longings. The mistake we often make is to believe that one individual or relationship will complete us, make us whole. But that's a myth. Each one of us is far more complicated and has needs much more varied than we might initially think. We thrive and grow more fully with the interaction, support, and love from a variety of people during our lives.

My wife and I have a wonderful relationship, but she also needs other people to make her life full and meaningful. Our two sons, Tyler and Jared, give Vicky the opportunity to experience motherhood. Her father and mother provide parental support and personal recollections that go back to before the crib. Her sisters Joanne and Sandy are her two best friends. And Wanda, Susan, and Janie are special friends with whom she laughs, shares, and cries. No one relationship can give you everything. You may need many healthy relationships to express and share all the diverse parts of yourself.

Relationships Will Die If Not Nurtured

Every relationship is a living entity. Like a plant or tree, each relationship has to be watered, pruned, and nurtured with loving care, or it will die. The grandfather who peers out his window in hopes of seeing your car in the driveway, the friend wishing for a reply to her letter, and the cousin waiting for your promised trip to the fishing hole are all like parched, brittle trees waiting for you to water them. Relationships cannot survive on their own. They require your participation, and they will die if not nurtured.

Relationships Are Both Pleasurable and Painful

Each of our love relationships is a journey into both heaven and hell. When we truly open our hearts to another person, we discover both pleasure and pain. As psychiatrist and author Elisabeth Kübler-Ross says, "Grief is the price we pay for loving." Although her observation describes the pain we experience with the loss of a loved one, it can also apply to the pain we feel when a loved one disappoints, frustrates, neglects, or misuses us during the course of the relationship.

Pleasure and pain are two sides of the same coin. Ultimately, you don't get one without the other. My friend Jeanette's son was an ideal child—courteous, mindful, and optimistic—who brought her great joy for the first thirteen years of his life. During the next six years, Scott caused Jeanette great pain with his rebelliousness, drug addiction, and petty criminal activities. Scott, now in his late twenties, is happily married, has a healthy daughter, and works in a job he enjoys. Scott is again a source of joy for his mother. Jeanette told me recently, "Scott really stretched my heart. I've never known such happiness or misery, and he was the source of both."

Relationships Require Flexibility

One certainty I can guarantee you about any relationship is this—relationships change. No healthy relationship remains the same forever because people change. We get older, more experienced. We learn new things about ourselves and life in general. Our comfort zones expand to encompass new territory, and things that used to frighten or intimidate us no longer pose the same threat. Because we've changed, the morning of a relationship is much different from the afternoon of the relationship. And it changes still in the twilight of life, because people change. Whether it's changing jobs, changing diapers, or changing opinions, each of us will continue to rethink, readjust, and reshape who we are.

Flexibility will make your journey through relationships more enjoyable and successful. Your willingness and ability to bend and adjust are essential in providing your relationship with the room to grow and develop as it should. Without flexibility, you will suffocate and strangle the bond that holds you and your loved one together.

As the ancient Chinese philosopher Lao-tzu reminded us in the *Tao Te Ching* twenty-five hundred years ago,

A tree that is unbending is easily broken
The hard and strong will fall
The soft and weak will overcome.

Yield to change and strive to remain flexible in your relationships with loved ones.

All relationships require giving. You cannot fully experience relationships without giving up some self-centeredness and focusing your attention and efforts on the people you love. Now that you have a basic understanding of relationships, let's begin the journey of becoming a gift giver with those you love. Let's begin with your first gift—your decision to give.

Deciding to Give

~

"Love is a decision, not a feeling."
–M. Scott Peck

The lights of the small town were beginning to twinkle yellow and soft against the dark backdrop of the Cascade Mountains in the distance. Bundled in my down parka, I surveyed the tiny village from a bench at the top of Pennsylvania Street and recalled fondly so many episodes of North-ern Exposure, *which were filmed right here in Roslyn, Washington.*

I was in Roslyn for three days, courtesy of my wife, who surprised me one Father's Day with a round-trip ticket to Seattle, two nights' motel stay in Roslyn, and a rental car. Vicky knew how much I enjoyed watch-ing reruns of the old CBS television series, how they spoke deeply to me with their quirky story lines of friendship, life, and joy.

This surprise trip came at a time when I was going through a minor depression. Nothing serious. Just a gray period when things don't go the way you had planned and life loses some detail and color. I remember opening the Father's Day card from Vicky and noticing only one plane ticket to Seattle.

"Aren't you going too?" I asked Vicky.

"No," she said, "I decided that a solo trip will speak to your heart more deeply. I'd love to go, but it will be better if you go alone. You go and have a wonderful time." And I did.

Those three days in Roslyn restored my spirit. No significant insights or life-changing revelations. Nothing I could put my finger on. Just a quiet, magical time of meals alone at the Roslyn Cafe, late-night coffee at the Brick Tavern, and watching the evening lights of this northern heaven from the bench at the end of Pennsylvania Street. I loved my journey to Roslyn. But I loved much more my wife's willingness to care for my soul and decision to give from her heart.

From the moment you entered this life, you began receiving from others. You received primarily from your **family of origin**—your primary parental and sibling group during the first eighteen years of life—but a constellation of others also participated to satisfy your physical, emotional, psychological, and spiritual needs. These people might include your grandparents, aunts and uncles, cousins, friends, neighbors, baby-sitters, and doctors. Without their care, you would have died within days. In essence, they gave you life by their giving.

After you have been loved, nurtured, and guided by these people during your childhood and adolescence, you develop the ability to live more independently of their support. With this independence comes the opportunity to be a source of love, nurture, and guidance to others. Instead of only receiving, you can begin to give, encourage, help, and love others.

The turning point in many people's lives is the moment they begin this journey from being a receiver to being a giver. Not everyone embarks on this journey. Those who do choose varying degrees of giving, which can depend on the person they give to, the situation, and their own circumstances. Some people decide to give early in life, others wait until the end of their lives, and some never choose to give.

THE JOURNEY OF GIVING

The journey begins with your decision to become a person who gives rather than a person who only receives. Your decision to become a giver rather than a receiver will enable you to experience honest, healthy, and lasting relationships with those you love.

For most of us, the decision to become a giver in our relationships is not a concept we are familiar with, or in many cases, even aware of. Let me give you an example. When I meet with a couple for premarital counseling, one of the first questions I ask each person is, "What are ten things your fiancé(e) loves about you?" The initial response from both men and women is usually "I don't know" or "I've never really thought about it before." Sometimes individuals respond humorously or even defensively, but rarely can people list even five behaviors or qualities they possess.

When I eventually pose the question "What are ten things you love about your fiancé(e)?" they respond much more readily and can usually list a number of qualities and skills they recognize and appreciate in their partner. "He really loves me," "She makes me laugh," "He's thoughtful," "She's attractive," "He's strong," and "She is a loving person" are common answers.

When the same questions are posed to parents and children in family therapy, their responses are similar. Both parents and children usually can identify one or two attributes or skills they love about other family members, but have difficulty identifying their own. Perhaps this can be explained by a reluctance to brag or speak positively about themselves. But after having worked with hundreds of individuals in therapy and in relationship classes, I believe this inability to identify positive skills and qualities in ourselves can be attributed to our deeply embedded preoccupation with what others can give us. We are often blinded by our desire to receive rather than to give.

The first step in improving relationships is the conscious decision to become someone who gives—someone who will focus on what he or she can provide the other person in a relationship rather than what he or she can get. This shift from self to other in relationships is the turning point in our lives, marking the change from childhood to adulthood.

As a symbol of your commitment to improve a relationship with a loved one, consider signing the following statement:

I choose to focus 50 percent of my attention and 50 percent of my efforts on giving gifts from the heart to _____
in our relationship. This process of giving involves specific communication behaviors I will learn, practice, and implement during the next ninety days in my efforts to improve our relationship.

_____

Your Signature

Often in therapy and in my relationship classes, people react to this contract with reluctance, doubt, and even suspicion. But I ask each individual to sign the contract nonetheless.

If an individual chooses not to sign the contract, I interpret that decision as an unwillingness to improve the relationship. Maybe the particular relationship is not worth the effort or energy. Maybe this is not the time for change in attitude or behavior. Whatever the reason, if the individual declines to sign the contract, I will still continue work with him or her, but my expectations and demands are modified to honor and accommodate the individual's decision to stay where he or she is for now. And that is okay!

If you choose not to sign the contract right now for whatever reason, that's okay. You can still benefit from reading the rest of this book because the gifts it contains might provide you with an entirely new and different way of regarding your relationships with others as well as your relationship with yourself. The gifts in this book might also expand and deepen your ideas of what is required of all healthy relationships and how you can develop and maintain your relationships. Who knows, after reading this book you might change your mind and become a giver of gifts in all your relationships.

If the individual chooses to sign the contract, the process of giving gifts from the heart begins at that moment and his or her relationship will begin to take a different path from that instant.

If you agree to the giving statement and are willing to commit to a program of giving communication gifts to a loved one, congratulations! You have taken the most important step in improving your relationship with a loved one. You've decided to begin the journey of giving gifts from the heart—gifts that will connect you to those you love.

Before we explore other gifts, I'd like to offer six guidelines that will make your giving easier.

GUIDELINES FOR GIVING

Any new process or approach needs some guidelines to keep us on track, to help us avoid pitfalls, and to ensure that we actually achieve what we set out to do. Here are six guidelines to keep in mind when giving the gifts presented in this book.

Try Softer

This is not a race or a contest. The purpose of giving is not to rack up points or dramatically change a relationship overnight. The goal is to give specific gifts of communication that will enable you to connect more deeply with those you love.

Each gift will serve to establish open, supportive, and authentic communication with those individuals in your life who mean something to you. Just as your current relationship with these people took months and years to establish, your new attitude of giving communication gifts will take time to implement. The fruits of your giving may not be evident immediately, so remember to take it slow and easy. Rather than trying harder, try softer.

One Gift at a Time

We have a tendency to go to extremes when we begin a new project, discover a new hobby, or find a new friend. The same is true here. My clients and students, in their enthusiasm, tend to want to put all of these gifts to use at one time. They will often overwhelm others with an avalanche of poorly executed new behaviors. Rather than learn to use one gift well, they try to share all of them at once, poorly.

Instead, try one gift for a week or two, even a month or two, before moving on to a new one. There's no rush. Each gift will demand its own special work or effort from you. Enjoy learning about and practicing each gift, one at a time. And enjoy the results that each gift may bring to the relationship. Take it one at a time.

Be Gentle on Yourself

The process of giving gifts from the heart does not require perfection. All I ask is that you try each gift with the attitude of wanting to give something to someone you love. That's all. Whether you do it perfectly or just good enough is not important. It's the direction of your heart that will eventually determine the success of each gift. Is your heart pointed in the direction of self? Or is your heart pointed in the direction of another? Striving for perfection not only places more pressure on you to perform in some unrealistic way, it will sabotage and undermine the way with which your giving will be received. Be gentle on yourself. You don't have to be perfect, you just have to try.

Take It Seriously

While you apply these gifts with a light touch, not expecting perfection from yourself or from the recipient, your intentions should be very serious. The purpose for which you are giving from the heart is to improve your heart—to intentionally shift your frame of reference from self to other, from taker to giver. This shift might be the most important goal you will achieve in this lifetime.

Beyond improved communication and deeper relationships with those you love, you may discover a part of you that is more loving, caring, and nurturing than you had previously known or experienced. You may find that you like, appreciate, and even enjoy yourself more than ever before.

In the end, you want to come to terms with yourself before you die. You want to come to a place where you can accept the life you had lived, without many regrets. To discover the truth that "we only really take that which we give away" is perhaps the most serious lesson we will ever learn. Life is about relationships, and this is serious business indeed.

Be Careful

When giving the gifts presented in this book, be careful. Don't try anything that makes you uncomfortable. You don't have to do anything you don't want. Perhaps in the future, you might want to try those gifts in a different relationship or under different circumstances. Who knows? Just remember that you decide. Don't push yourself too much or too quickly.

Be careful not to use these gifts to manipulate, coerce, or victimize others. Each gift possesses great potential to influence not only how others communicate with you, but also how they feel toward you. Be ethical in your application of these gifts. Consider the safety, feelings, and appropriate boundaries of others as you give these gifts.

Also, you don't want to encourage any co-dependent behavior where you are doing all the giving in a relationship and receiving absolutely nothing in return. You don't want to paint yourself into a corner and reinforce a relationship where the recipient of your gifts wants only more and more of your effort, without also giving to you. Limit or refuse giving these gifts to any person who is alcoholically or chemically dependent, is verbally or physically abusive to you or others, or desires more from the relationship than you are willing to give. Giving has its limits and you need to be sensitive and aware of your feelings and intuitions.

Give Joyfully

Give with an attitude of joy, for the gifts you give are tangible acts of love that not only bless the receiver, but you, the giver, as well. Don't give from an attitude of obligation or duty. Smile, hum, and skip a step or two before you deliver one of these gifts to a loved one. Your joyful attitude alone is enough to change a relationship for the better. Be of good cheer. Give joyfully.

BEGIN THE JOURNEY OF GIVING

Something magical happens when one individual in a relationship changes—the other person in the relationship also changes. Not immediately. Not dramatically. But over time, a change always occurs. No relationship remains the same when one person adopts a new attitude or new behavior. Giving gifts from the heart can promote relationships in which the same gifts will be returned to you.

By deciding to give rather than to receive, you will change not only those you give to, you will experience changes in yourself as well. You'll see your romantic partner, family members, and friends through new eyes because you'll be looking to give rather than to receive. You'll be watching for opportunities to accept, connect, and listen to others. You'll be on the lookout for chances to encourage, touch, and forgive those you love. You'll experience the lightness and freedom that can come only from putting others first and yourself second. You'll discover an inner calmness and peace that you hadn't experienced when you were struggling to get what you thought you needed to be happy. You'll find that in giving, you will receive all that you need to experience more loving relationships.

To prepare you to give, this book will explore the importance of each gift, outline specific ways to communicate and share each gift, and suggest guidelines for implementing each gift. All of the gifts presented in this book will be fun and exciting to share with those you love. But each gift will demand from you a spirit of giving.

Without your decision to become a giver in your relationships, the chances of connecting and deepening your current and future relationships are severely limited. It is only when you decide to give do you begin to experience lasting, loving relationships. Even a journey of ten thousand miles begins with one step. Your decision to give is the first step in the journey of giving gifts from the heart. I hope you will accept this invitation.

⌒

1.1 Personal Exploration: If You Are Undecided to Give

If you are undecided about giving gifts from the heart in a particular relationship, or perhaps in any relationship, you most likely have good reasons for your indecision or reluctance. You know best. But rather than tossing this book out the window or beginning the next chapter, you might want to explore the following questions. Your responses may help you gain some clarification and insight into your decision.

Of which individual are you thinking when you consider giving gifts from the heart? _____

What are the benefits of your relationship with this person?

_____

_____

_____

What specific gifts (such as communicating for connection, accepting you, listening for understanding, asking questions, enlarging you, flowing with conflict, showing he or she cares, encouraging your growth, and forgiving you) does he or she give you?

_____

_____

Why don't you want to give gifts to him or her?

_____

_____

_____

What do you think would happen if you decide to give him or her these gifts?

_____

_____

_____

What do you think would happen if you decide not to give him or her these gifts?

_____

_____

_____

How do you feel about your response to the previous question?

_____

_____

_____

1.2 Practice Giving: Sharing Your Decision to Give

If you have decided to focus some attention and effort into giving gifts from the heart, congratulations! Now that you have made the decision, you need to communicate it to your loved one.

Take five to ten minutes to meet with your loved one at a convenient time and in a location where you will not be disturbed. Tell your loved one that you have made a decision to give more to him or her. Ask your loved one the following questions:

1. How can I love you more?
2. What can I do to show you more respect?
3. What can I do to increase our intimacy?
4. What can I do to increase your feeling of security?
5. What can I do to encourage you more?

The answers to these questions will provide you with a great deal of information about the specific things you can give your loved one. Whatever your loved one says, don't evaluate, defend, or attack. Just listen to his or her responses. Most likely, the answers your loved one gives to you can be satisfied by many of the gifts outlined in this book.

1.3   Practice Giving: Celebrating Your Decision to Give

After you have listened to your loved one give you feedback on the five questions you asked, take him or her out for a meal, a walk, or some other special activity to celebrate your decision to give gifts from the heart. This celebration will mark the beginning of a new relationship for you and your loved one. And I hope it will be the first of many wonderful celebrations you will enjoy together. Congratulations for making the decision to give!

Communicating for Connection

∽

"Our willingness to connect with others
determines the quality of our lives."
–May Sarton

Three dark figures walked slowly from my office toward the parking lot. I couldn't see their faces on that warm June evening, but I knew the husband, the wife, and their twelve-year-old son were smiling just the same.

The greatest reward I receive as a counselor is to watch individuals behave more lovingly toward others and themselves. This family had taken a significant step in that direction because the husband had chosen to communicate for connection rather than for competition.

During the family's first two therapy sessions, I noticed that the father dominated the discussions by directing criticism at his wife and son. He would compete for my attention by constantly interrupting his wife and son, and he would often criticize my suggestions and comments.

At the conclusion of the second session, I told the husband, "You have two choices whenever you open your mouth. You can communicate for competition and criticism. Or you can communicate for connection. The first choice will make life miserable for your family, me, and yourself. The second will make life enjoyable for everyone, yourself included. The choice is always yours." I ended our session on that statement.

Then something miraculous happened. The husband changed his behavior. He didn't change immediately and he didn't change completely, but he did change. The husband still interrupted and criticized occasion-

ally, but not nearly as often. He participated willingly, even enthusiastically. By the end of the fifth hour of therapy, he had not only told his wife and son he loved them, he also told me I had changed his life.

"I never had someone tell me I actually had a choice in how I talked," he admitted. *"My dad always yelled and criticized us when I was growing up, so I guess I just sort of did the same with my family. But I don't want to be miserable. And I don't want my family to be unhappy either. So, I'm trying to communicate for connection."*

And, he still communicates for connection with his family, more than three years after that warm June evening.

∽

How do you usually communicate? From my observations, I'm convinced that the majority of our communication with others is evaluative in nature. That is, we judge or evaluate just about everything that is shared with us: "I agree," "I disagree," "That's good," "That's bad," "You're wrong," "You're right." The list goes on forever. This is **communicating for competition,** where we actually compete for who is right and who is wrong. Communication for competition separates us from one another. It builds walls, not bridges.

Communicating for connection is not about victory, control, or mastery. The goal is not to win an argument, criticize an opponent, or even report the facts. The primary purpose of communicating for connection is the linking of hearts and the joining of souls. Occasionally you may have a difference of opinion to air, a criticism to share, or a conflict to resolve. But the primary intent and focus of communicating for connection is to join you with those you love and establish ties that will withstand the tugging of differences, conflict, and distance.

Linguist and author Deborah Tannen asserts that men communicate for competition rather than connection. They communicate to persuade, to convince, to argue, and to win. Men aren't the only ones who are rewarded for these skills. Women are assuming increasingly more of the persuasive, assertive, and motivational communication skills so they can more effectively compete in the workplace. These communication skills are essential to getting the job done and the objectives achieved; but in matters of the heart, they are more often the primary cause of relational conflict, frustration, and misunderstanding. If it works on the job, it doesn't necessarily work at home. We need to learn and give the gift of communicating for connection to bond with loved ones.

As someone wisely observed, "On your deathbed, you won't wish you had spent more time at the office." If anything, you will regret not having spent more time with your loved ones. For it is your relationships and deep connections with others that gives life its meaning.

On our deathbeds, very few of us will be consoled by clutching our diplomas, bank statements, or deeds of trust. Most of us would rather spend our final moments holding the hand of someone we have loved and has loved us in return. This is how we would like to end our life journey.

But how do we get to that point? And more important, how can we live our lives every day so we can experience more loving relationships now? The answer, I believe, lies in learning and practicing the skills that connect us with others.

COMPONENTS OF COMMUNICATION

Before we explore specific ways to communicate for connection, let's look at the components of communication—the building blocks of connection. To begin with, we will define communication. For our purposes, we will use one of the simplest definitions I know.

Communication is the sending and receiving of messages. Essentially, it is the process of putting your thoughts and feelings into words and behaviors that will be accurately received and understood by another person. The communication process also involves your accurate reception of the other person's words and behaviors so you can understand his thoughts and feelings. Communication is the only way we can relate to each other. Without communication, a relationship is impossible. To better understand the communication process, let's examine its four primary components.

Participants

Without the individuals who are communicating messages to one another, there is no communication process. People are the reason for communication. Each individual in the communication event is both the sender and the receiver of messages, often at the same time. We are the participants of communication.

Messages

The second component of the communication process is the message. Messages that are communicated between participants can be either thoughts or feelings, such as the thought "Let's go now" or the feeling "I'm happy." Messages can contain both thoughts and feelings in the same statement, such as "I'm happy we're going now." Messages are like the paintings of the mind and the heart. The purpose of communication is to convey these images of thought and feeling accurately.

But the meaning of the words that represent these images—these thoughts and feelings—is not in the words themselves, but in the people who send and receive them. The symbol or word "love" does not "mean" the same thing to different people. The images the word "love" can evoke in the minds of people are as varied as the individuals themselves. For one person "love" means romance, for another sex, and for yet another, manipulation. Meaning is in people and not in words. To better understand this concept, we'll examine the third component of communication.

Encoding/Decoding

When someone wants to communicate the message "I love you," he will have to encode that feeling into words and behaviors he believes will most accurately convey his message. "I love you," "I want to be yours," "You turn me on," and "I want to be with you" are all possibilities he may consider to communicate his feeling. He decides which is best.

But words are just the beginning of the encoding process. He must now decide how to communicate the message. The nonverbal categories of sound, sight, touch, smell, and taste are all possibilities. He could whisper or shout his message. He could scribble it on the back of a hamburger wrapper or have it plastered on a billboard. He could also convey his message with a gentle hug, the scent of cologne, or the taste of homemade cookies. The encoding process involves decisions on the part of the sender, who determines the content and form a message will take.

Once the message has been sent, the receiver begins the decoding process. How is the content and form of the message interpreted? That is determined by a number of variables. The receiver's physical abilities, psychological makeup, and emotional state are just a few of the many factors that contribute to the decoding process. Interpretation of a simple note stating "I love you" depends on the receiver's eyesight, personal definition of the word "love," current emotional state, and location where the note is read. These are just a few simple variables that influence and determine the receiver's decoding process. The process begins anew when the receiver assumes the sending role and encodes her message of response.

Context

All of this complicated encoding/decoding of messages by the participants in the communication event occurs within a certain context, which is the fourth communication component.

The context takes into account the cultural, historical, and social climate of the event. "I love you" scribbled on a Hallmark card may be acceptable in America, but in Japan, such a direct statement of affection may be considered impolite or rude. If the sender has a known history of sending these cards to anyone with a mailbox, the message could easily be discounted. But if the sender has a history of reticent behavior, his message could take on greater meaning. Finally, if the card is received after an argument, it could be interpreted differently than if it were received after an enjoyable meal. The context within which the message is sent plays an important role in the reception and interpretation of the message.

The communication process at first glance may appear simple and straightforward, but as you've seen, the various components of this process suggest a much more involved and complicated system of sending and receiving messages. To keep communication as specific and clear as possible, we need to claim ownership of our statements.

OWN YOUR COMMUNICATION—I-STATEMENTS

Whenever we communicate to another person, it is important that our messages be as specific and clear as possible. To avoid confusion and ambiguity, we need to use **I-statements,** which allow you to own your thoughts and feelings. It is your ownership of messages that enables you to effectively express who you are. Here are some examples of I-statements:

I want to live in the country.
I like the rain.
I think you are intelligent.
It's **my** opinion that it's better to own a home than rent a home.

Each of these I-statements shows speaker ownership. Did you notice how an I-statement doesn't necessarily have to contain the word "I?" For example, "It's my opinion that it's better to own a home than rent a home" is an I-statement because it shows ownership by the word "my."

I-statements provide several advantages. First, an I-statement lets the receiver of the message know who owns or originated the thought or idea. If I-statements are not used, ownership of the message may be uncertain or overstated. Look at the following examples of non-I-statements:

Most people want to live in the country.
Everybody likes the rain.
All of the class thinks you're intelligent.
People believe it's better to own a home than rent a home.

Compare these four non-I-statements to the four I-statements. Do you get a different feeling from the I-statements? I-statements show ownership of the thought or feeling, whereas non-I-statements do not.

The second advantage of I-statements is that they provide a target for the receiver of the message to respond. If a speaker says, "Everybody likes the rain," the receiver might be less likely to disagree, because the source of the message and the target of a rebuttal is then "everybody" rather than the speaker. It's as if the entire world ("everybody") was standing behind the speaker, supporting her opinion. If the speaker owned the opinion by using an I-statement ("I believe everybody likes the rain"), the receiver might be more likely to disagree or discuss the matter.

The third advantage of I-statements is that they prevent people from speaking for others. This often happens in relationships where members are too close or enmeshed for healthy functioning. Listen for the unhealthy tone of the following statements in which the speaker actually "speaks" for others:

Sarah feels it's important for us to discuss our problems.
My boyfriend always tells me I should go back to school.
My parents are excited about our future.
My boss thinks you're unfair.

I-statements would prevent these types of remarks from occurring.

The fourth advantage of I-statements is that they offer more thought-ful statements. Because they show ownership, I-statements force the speaker to weigh remarks more cautiously. It's easier to flippantly say, "**Everyone really likes you**," rather than own the statement and say, "**I like you**." When I require my students and clients to use I-statements, they generally respond more slowly (perhaps suggesting more thoughtful remarks) and softly.

The final advantage of I-statements is that they discourage blaming others. Many times we use what is called "you-statements" instead of I-statements. We send "you" messages such as:

You make me upset.
You talk too much.
You're a grouch.

You-statements can be messages of condemnation, which direct blame to the receiver. If the speaker used I-statements instead, he would be required to own more of the message rather than shifting all the blame to the receiver ("you"). Notice the shift in ownership and clarity when the same three statements are recast as I-statements:

I get upset when you call me "honey." (You make me upset.)
I noticed you've been speaking for twenty minutes. (You talk too much.)
I see you're not smiling again. (You're a grouch.)

Do you see how I-statements change the tone of each statement? The I-statements have less of a blaming and faultfinding tone. They emphasize the speaker's perceptions and feelings, not the receiver's. Once again, I-statements show ownership of opinions and feelings. The I-statement is the fundamental building block of the messages we send. Remember to own your statements when you communicate for connection.

LEVELS OF COMMUNICATION

Now that we know how to construct an I-statement, the next step in the process of communicating for connection is to examine the four levels of communication: surface talk, reporting facts, giving opinions, and sharing feelings.

Each level represents a different type of information, which in turn represents a different degree of intimacy in how information is shared. In surface talk, the speaker provides little personal information and merely acknowledges the other person with some pleasantry or greeting. In reporting facts, the speaker conveys information that can be verified or proven. In giving opinions, the speaker discloses beliefs, attitudes, or opinions. In sharing feelings, the speaker communicates at the deepest level—the relating of emotions. True connections with loved ones occur at the feeling level.

During the course of one conversation, we can communicate at all four levels of communication. Yet most of our conversations are limited to the less personal levels of surface talk, reporting facts, and giving opinions. We generally reserve sharing feelings with individuals we trust.

If we have talked with someone at the surface level and find it satisfactory, we generally venture to the next level—reporting facts. If the listener then betrays our trust by gossiping about information we have disclosed, we would tend not to communicate with the individual at this level again. In fact, we would probably restrict communication to the surface talk level, if we even talk to the person at all. We don't usually go to the next level of disclosure until we trust the other person at the present level. Let's examine the four levels of sharing in more detail.

Level 1: Surface Talk
In the first level of communication, we keep our conversations to minimal disclosure. The surface talk level includes greetings, casual acknowledgment of strangers and acquaintances, chitchat with coworkers, and so forth. The primary goal is to acknowledge another individual without providing any personal information about ourselves. Listen to the following surface level remarks:

Nice to see you! / You too!
How's it going? / Fine. How about you? / Great!
Take it easy. / See you around!

The purpose of surface talk is to acknowledge another person in a socially acceptable manner, not to conduct some deep, involved conversation with them.

Level 2: Reporting Facts

The next level of communication involves the disclosing of facts. Introducing yourself at a party, remarking that you've won a lottery, and telling your roommate that the dishes have been washed are all examples of reporting factual information. The key to identifying communication at this level is that the content of messages can be verified or proven. Here are examples of reporting facts:

> My blood pressure is 170/95.
> We have dinner reservations for 8:00 P.M.
> I have a gift for you in the garage.
> I've been clean and sober for three years.

Reporting factual information about yourself can be important in connecting with those you love. It's the level of communication at which you begin to share who you are.

Level 3: Giving Opinions

The next deeper level of communication is giving opinions. This level is a little riskier than reporting facts. By giving your opinions about topics, people, or events, you are exposing more of who you are. You are allowing others to see your opinions, attitudes, and beliefs. This can be much more threatening because there is a greater chance of disagreement, disapproval, and conflict brought about by the differences of opinion.

Disagreement is natural. We couldn't possibly agree on every topic we discuss with others. And we wouldn't want to. That's the beauty of being in relationships. It's often our differences that make people attractive to us. These differences add to us, complement our weaknesses, and show us new ways of seeing, thinking, and feeling.

The development of trust is essential in sharing opinions. Trust is something you build by sharing your opinions with others and believing they will hear your opinions, share their own, and discuss the differences in an atmosphere of safety and acceptance. Here are examples of opinions:

> I **believe** I could learn to fly an airplane.
> I **think** our relationship can work.
> I **predict** my parents will give you the money.

Level 4: Sharing Feelings

The deepest level of communication is the sharing of feelings. The communication of facts and opinions paints a two-dimensional figure of who we are; the sharing of feelings provides our loved ones with a three-dimensional person to connect to. It's at the sharing feelings level that people really communicate for connection.

Although women are usually much more willing to communicate at the feeling level, men can also be encouraged to share their emotions with loved ones. Here are three ways to communicate feelings with those you love—direct feeling statements, explanation feeling statements, and picture feeling statements.

Direct feeling statements. The most basic way to communicate a feeling is to use a direct feeling statement, which is an I-statement containing a feeling word. Here are some examples:

I feel delighted.
I'm feeling sad.
I'm proud of you.
I love you.

Explanation feeling statements. The second way to share a feeling is with an explanation feeling statement. In this statement, you not only own the feeling, you also include information about the feeling. In the following examples, I have divided each statement into the direct feeling statement and the explanation for the feeling.

I'm happy / because you took the day off.
I've felt embarrassed / ever since I gave that speech.
I feel so exuberant / after completing my cross-country trip.
I feel ashamed / that I broke my promise to you.

Did you notice how explanation feeling statements provide more information for the receiver of the message? You don't always have to include an explanation for your feelings. In fact, because feelings are not rational or logical, many times you might not have a reason or explanation for feeling a certain way. If that's the case, you can simply say, "I'm feeling upset and I don't know why." What's important in any case is that you begin to share your feelings with those you love. It's the primary means of communicating for connection.

Picture feeling statements. The third way you can share a feeling is with a **simile**—a description using the words "as if" or "like." Similes often provide the receiver with a different way of hearing or processing your feeling statement. Read these examples of picture feeling statements and see if your response differs from the direct feeling statements that follow in parentheses.

I feel *like* I'm floating on a cloud.   (I feel relaxed.)
I feel *as if* I'm chained to my desk.   (I'm feeling overworked.)

The wonderful thing about these picture feeling statements is that they provide a visual description of the feeling you are experiencing. They also can open up different channels of communication between you and your loved ones.

The four levels of communication provide an understanding of how we connect verbally with those we love. Although reporting facts and giving opinions are vital to successful communication, it is the sharing of your emotional life—your feelings—that deepens and strengthens your relationships. Without your willingness and ability to communicate at this fourth level of communication, your relationships will lack intimacy and depth.

Throughout the book we will explore specific methods and techniques to encourage communication at the three deeper levels of communication discussed in this section. The most important thing to keep in mind when communicating for connection is that your attitude and your desire to connect are more important than any technique or skill. With this in mind, let's look at the goals of the LINK Process of communicating for connection.

THE LINK PROCESS

Whether I'm working with clients in therapy or students in classes, I have them keep four fundamental desires in mind no matter what communication gift they are giving. These four desires, which help preserve the spirit and attitude of communicating for connection, are summarized in the acronym LINK.

Listen
Invite
Notice
Know

Listen: The Desire to Listen

Theologian Paul Tillich maintains that "the first duty of love is to listen." And unlike communicating for competition, with its emphasis on projective verbal skills, the first duty of communicating for connection is the receptive skills of listening, being open, and attempting to understand the thoughts and feelings of others. To really listen to other individuals may be one of the most difficult and demanding activities we can undertake. But we can never truly begin to connect with other people without a desire to listen to what they have to share.

Invite: The Desire to Invite

The second desire necessary in communicating for connection is that of wanting the other to open up to us and share thoughts and feelings, concerns and dreams, hurts and triumphs. Communicating for connection requires a deep desire to invite other people into our lives, to welcome them into our homes, and to make a place for them in our hearts. We need to communicate to them in word and deed that they are invited into our lives. They should feel a spirit of hospitality and even of homecoming in our presence. We should greet those we wish to develop relationships with a posture of warmth, acceptance, and excitement. We need to issue these invitations to a relationship.

Notice: The Desire to Notice

The third desire is to pay attention, notice, and acknowledge those people we want in our lives. M. Scott Peck, author of *The Road Less Traveled,* believes that if you really love someone or something, you will give that person or object your full attention. The example he cites is the love a young boy might have for his first car. The boy spends time with it, washes and waxes it, and even sleeps in the backseat of the car because he cannot stand being away from the object of his love! Now that's passion.

Well, you might not want to go that far. But you need to pay attention to those people you love. If you really want to know what a person loves, observe how that person spends his or her money and time. To communicate for connection requires that we pay attention to those we love.

KNOW: The Desire to Know

All this desire and effort required for communicating for connection is worthless if we don't know whom we're connected to. We need a strong desire to know the person we are in a relationship with. What's the point of giving all these gifts from the heart if we don't know the person in whom we're investing this effort?

Before I met my wife, I once dated a woman who never called me by my first name. During our three dates, she never asked me one substantive question about myself. I don't know if she was capable of engaging in dialogue. Maybe she really wasn't interested in me at all as a person, because she never quit talking about herself. Those were three of the most miserable evenings of my life. The desire to want to know someone, to take an interest in discovering the deeper thoughts, feelings, and dreams of another person is essential in a relationship.

GUIDELINES FOR COMMUNICATING FOR CONNECTION

As you give the gift of communicating for connection, keep in mind the following five guidelines: increase I-statement use gradually; share your opinions and feelings appropriately; don't force others to disclose; be able to keep a secret; and be happy rather than right.

Increase I-Statement Use Gradually

Many times, my students and clients go overboard when they begin to increase their use of I-statements in their everyday conversations. They delight in taking ownership of their thoughts and feelings, but tend to overwhelm and confuse their loved ones rather than connect with them. Overuse of I-statements also can be perceived as a self-centered way of communicating. So increase your I-statement use gradually. Be sensitive to the needs of others to express their thoughts and feelings, too. Keep balanced—speak *and* listen.

Share Your Opinions and Feelings Appropriately

Sharing feelings and opinions is important to establish and maintain intimate connections with your loved ones. Whether a romantic partner, family member, or close friend, your opinions and feelings enable other people to know who you are, what you believe, and how you feel. That same information may not necessarily be appropriate or interesting to people with whom you interact daily, such as the grocery store cashier, bus driver, or plumber. Make sure that you disclose personal information only to people who are truly important in your life.

Don't Force Others to Disclose

You may discover that sharing opinions and feelings with others becomes easier with practice. But don't make the mistake of thinking that your loved ones share a similar ability or willingness to disclose personal information. They may not, no matter how open you've become. As you communicate for connection, don't try to coerce others to share their opinions and feelings. You cannot force another person to do something. You can only share your truth and invite them to do the same with you. By not trying to force them to share, you create an open space in which they can relax, breathe, and maybe even change. Be patient.

Be Able to Keep a Secret

As your loved ones disclose personal information to you, be careful not to violate their trust by telling others what you have found out. Keep their personal information to yourself. Even if you think your loved ones would not mind your sharing the information, don't. It's better to err on the side of preserving someone's privacy rather than disclosing information without permission and having to apologize later. What you consider public information might be private to your loved ones. Preserve your relationships by being able to keep a secret.

Be Happy Rather Than Right

A relationship is not a debate. The purpose of communicating for connection is not to win or prove that you're right. The purpose is to establish lines of communication and avenues of meeting where you can get to know and appreciate the thoughts and feelings of other people. So what if you don't agree on everything. Big deal if you have different opinions about certain issues. It's these differences that make your relationships more interesting, refreshing, and stimulating. Don't view communicating as a debate or contest with a winner or loser. See it as a means of getting to know another person.

As you communicate in your relationships, remember that your primary goal is communication for connection, not competition. Rather than argue, persuade, or critique those you love, connect with them. By owning your statements and sharing your opinions and feelings, you can more effectively connect with others and give them something to connect to. Give the gift of connection to those you love.

~

2.1 **Personal Exploration: Is It Connection or Competition?**

Before you begin to give the gift of communicating for connection, let's make certain you learned the difference between statements that connect and statements that compete or evaluate. Read the following sentences and then mark an X next to those sentences that communicate for competition and mark an O next to those sentences that communication for connection.

1. _____ I think you're wrong for these three reasons...

2. _____ You're not as good with money as my mom. You'll be broke soon.

3. _____ I love you.

4. _____ You always interrupt me with stupid questions. Quit it!

5. _____ I'm so sure! You never help me when I have problems!

6. _____ How can I make you feel more comfortable when we're talking?

7. _____ I appreciate your thoughtfulness.

(3, 6, and 7 communicate for connection)

2.2 Personal Exploration: Connecting Behaviors

List three individuals from your life you feel are effective in their efforts to connect with you. Identify one specific behavior they demonstrate that makes you feel they are trying to connect rather than compete with you.

1. _____ connects with me by _____.

2. _____ connects with me by _____.

3. _____ connects with me by _____.

2.3 Practice Giving: Showing Your Connection

Select one individual from your life with whom you would like to connect at a deeper level during the next week. List two specific positive opinions or feelings you want to share with him or her, such as "I appreciate your thoughtfulness" or "I'm glad we're friends." Finally, set a tentative date by which you will communicate these opinions or feelings.

Name of individual you want to connect with: _____

List two opinions or feelings you want to share.

1. _____

2. _____

Date by which you will share these statements: _____

Accepting Others

❧

"To accept people as they are is to encourage
them to be better than they are."
–Carl Rogers

As far back as I can remember, people have always sought out my mother,
Helen. Young and old, male and female, family and friends, even strangers have gone out of their way to spend an hour or a few minutes with her.

My mom has been the one to whom countless people have come over
the years when they needed reassurance, support, or just a listening ear.
Whether it's the vice president of the company where she works or a
young, single mother in the neighborhood, people seek her out.

I think it's because she truly accepts people. She makes no effort to
judge or evaluate, to impress or influence, to rescue or change. Somehow
she's willing, as she says, to "accept others just as they are and love them
all the same." Just loving them is enough. Maybe that's why people seek
her out.

When I was in high school, one of Mom's friends asked if her teen-
age daughter could live with our family for a month because the girl's
lying and emotional outbursts had become unbearable for her parents.
After the girl had been with us for a few days, I complained that our
visitor hadn't changed one bit because she was yelling and complaining
just like before.

"That's okay, Randy," my mom replied. "It doesn't matter if she never
changes. I just want her to feel loved while she's here."

I continued my objections, but Mom only smiled. "And Randy, it's okay if you're upset," she said as she hugged me.

⤸

Psychologist and author Sheldon Kopp has suggested that the best way for a therapist to regard a patient is to love him, even if he doesn't ever change during the course of therapy. This rare acceptance of the patient, Kopp feels, creates an environment wherein the patient, perhaps for the first time in his life, is truly free of demands, ultimatums, and expectations. And it is within this environment that he might actually experience change.

I believe that acceptance is not only the first requirement for a therapeutic relationship between counselor and client, it is also the first requirement for any love relationship. To establish the foundation of a healthy relationship, we must be willing to give the gift of acceptance.

Let's define **acceptance** as "receiving what is." This might sound somewhat strange, to receive what is, but you do it all the time. For example, when you watch a beautiful sunset, you are receiving what is. You are accepting the sunset just the way it presents itself to you. There's no judging, fixing, changing, controlling, adjusting, teaching, redirecting, rejecting, blaming, insulting, criticizing, helping, or manipulating the sunset. You don't yell out for more red and less purple. You don't blame it for the cooling temperature of the air. And surely, you don't try to stop the sun from setting. There's just an "Ah, how beautiful." You just receive what is.

Much of our enjoyment of nature, music, literature, theater, and art is just receiving and enjoying what is. The enjoyment comes from accepting those things the way they are, exactly how they present themselves. Yet when it comes to people, especially those we love, it's often another matter. Rather than simply accept them—receive them just the way they are— we often judge, fix, blame, control, help, criticize, or manipulate them.

There are many reasons why we might have difficulty accepting those we love. One reason is that we were not accepted in our family of origin. Instead of being approved of and adequately loved, we experienced toxic amounts of criticism, control, and rejection. Another reason is our wish to control others. The need to dominate a relationship is not uncommon, and withholding acceptance and inflicting criticism are two ways to control another person. The final reason we might have difficulty accepting others is that we have difficulty accepting ourselves. It's difficult to love or accept another if we first haven't loved or accepted ourselves.

In relationships, we need to accept things about others that we might not agree with, find desirable, or even like. We need to accept our partner's idiosyncratic habits, our parents' odd attitudes, our friends' inexplicable behaviors. If we don't, and continue to evaluate, criticize, and try to control their thoughts and behaviors, we will only alienate ourselves from them. We must learn to become more open to their ideas, behaviors, and attitudes, or forever be at odds with our loved ones, ourselves, and the world.

NONVERBAL SIGNS OF ACCEPTANCE

To give the gift of acceptance is the first step in establishing and maintaining a healthy relationship. Without some degree of acceptance, a relationship cannot even begin. Can you imagine what it would be like to initiate a conversation with someone who frowns and looks away every time you try to speak? Can you imagine what it would be like to talk and have that person respond with labored sighs of disgust and disapproval? This wouldn't be an enjoyable experience. Who needs this?

The way you communicate nonverbally sets the tone of acceptance or rejection long before you speak. Your physical presence, noninterference, posture and gestures, eye contact, facial expressions, nodding, and tone of voice are examples of **nonverbal communication**—all communication that is not spoken or written. Let's briefly discuss each way you can nonverbally communicate acceptance.

Physical Presence
The most obvious way you can nonverbally communicate your acceptance of another person is by showing up, whether at a restaurant to meet an aunt or at the library for a friend's poetry reading. Your mere presence communicates your acceptance. Your absence is also a powerful nonverbal message. If you really accept someone, you will honor your promises to be with them.

Noninterference
Your acceptance of another person's behavior can be communicated by your doing nothing—your noninterference in his activity or behavior. Sim-

ply letting a loved one engage in a specific activity or follow a course of action, without interference, can be a sign of acceptance. To let your girl-friend engage in a hobby she enjoys or to smile as your dad leaves for his first date after his divorce is a powerful way to communicate acceptance.

Posture and Gestures

How you stand and sit can communicate acceptance or rejection. Facing away from someone or speaking over your shoulder can communicate re-jection; whereas facing the person directly can communicate acceptance. A slouched, withdrawn posture can communicate negative messages, whereas an erect posture or one where you lean toward the person can communicate positive messages. Your arms and hands can also convey ac-ceptance. Keep them open when speaking instead of crossing your arms or balling your hands into fists when being addressed. Be aware of what your body and gestures are communicating.

Eye Contact

Eye contact can communicate acceptance in this culture. To refuse to look at someone can be interpreted as a sign of rejection. Your eye contact can be a sign of acknowledgment and acceptance, especially when accompa-nied by a smile. When someone is speaking to you, use eye contact to demonstrate your interest and involvement. Don't look away or close your eyes and fall sleep. Remember, maintain eye contact when communicat-ing with others.

Facial Expressions

Your face says a lot about you. The old African warning "Watch the face, not the words" is supported by recent studies in credibility. When con-fronted with positive verbal messages and negative facial expressions, re-spondents assigned more credence to the facial expressions when asked to interpret them. If you are trying to communicate acceptance, remember to show appropriate facial expressions such as a smile. Your facial expres-sions are vitally important to your communication of acceptance.

Nodding

This isn't nodding-off-to-sleep nodding. This is acknowledgment nodding. The occasional nodding of your head is an encouraging nonverbal message that shows you are paying attention and acknowledging the words of the speaker. Don't overdo this nodding behavior, but use it to say, "I hear you" and "What you're saying is important."

Tone of Voice

It's not what you say that's important but rather how you say it. The statement "I love you" can mean a variety of things, depending on whether the words are spoken in a sarcastic, sincere, uncertain, or dominating tone of voice. To communicate acceptance, your voice should be pleasant, sincere, and gentle. Keep in mind that your tone of voice communicates the spirit of your heart.

VERBAL SIGNS OF ACCEPTANCE

In addition to the nonverbal signs of acceptance, there are a number of verbal ways to communicate your acknowledgment and acceptance of others. These verbal signs of acceptance are silence, nonevaluative listening, words of acceptance, phrases of acceptance, and invitations to share.

Silence

Two people cannot speak at the same time and expect communication to occur. By definition, communication is the sending and receiving of messages. Whenever someone speaks, someone else needs to listen in order for communication to occur. I believe most of us would rather speak than listen. So your willingness not to interrupt is a sign of acceptance. Your willingness to remain silent when another person is talking is a sign of love. To permit the other person to share, explore, and grow in your presence is to love the other.

Nonevaluative Listening

Nonevaluative listening reflects your decision to be silent and to listen to what the other person is saying, without interrupting with an evaluation or judgment. Many people can remain silent for ten or fifteen seconds, but not for much longer. "No way, you're wrong!" "That's a terrible thing to say," "You're absolutely correct," and "What a wonderful idea" are examples of negative and positive evaluations that punctuate even the best conversations after only a few seconds.

With nonevaluative listening, however, the listener remains silent for one, two, and even three minutes. The listener can smile, nod his head, lean into the speaker, and shift posture, but he does not verbally interrupt the speaker or add to the speaker's words. The speaker is free to explore her thoughts and feelings in the presence of another person without the usual verbal interruptions that characterize most of our conversations.

The first few times a speaker experiences your nonevaluative listening, she might ask, "Is there something wrong?" or "Are you mad at me?" These questions reflect her uneasiness with this new experience of not being interrupted or verbally evaluated by a listener. She is usually interrupted verbally every ten or twelve seconds, so your one to two minutes of silent attention can be uncomfortable or unnerving.

Your response should simply be, "Nothing's wrong. I'm just trying to hear what you have to say." Your nonevaluative listening will require some getting used to, but it will eventually invite deeper levels of communication between you and your loved one.

Verbal Responses of Acceptance

Words or phrases such as "Oh," "Um," "Really?" "Okay," "I see," "Is that so?" "That's interesting," and "Say more" are some verbal responses of acceptance. They are not evaluations of right or wrong, good or bad, or agreement or disagreement. They are intended to communicate your attentiveness and acceptance of what is being shared. It is your way to cheer your loved ones on, as if to say, "Keep going, you're doing a great job sharing!"

Invitations to Share

If you feel that a loved one wants to share but is reluctant, there are some things you can say to invite him to do so. The simplest invitation is "How's it going?" This invitation is relatively neutral and gives the person the choice to accept or to decline. Either way he responds to your invitation, honor his decision. If he decides to talk, listen nonevaluatively. If he declines, accept that also. What's important is that you invited him to share. Other invitations to share are:

> Tell me about it.
> Would you like to talk about your situation?

I'm interested in your point of view.
Sometimes it's good to share. I'd like to listen.

These are just a few ways you can encourage someone to open up. Many times people don't share because they feel no one wants to listen. Your invitations will let them know you want to listen and accept what they have to share.

GUIDELINES FOR ACCEPTING OTHERS

Whether your acceptance of others is expressed verbally or nonverbally, it provides a powerful invitation for relationship with another person. As you give the gift of accepting others, consider these guidelines: be more accepting of yourself; learn to float again; don't accept unacceptable behavior; and express your thoughts and feelings, too.

Be More Accepting of Yourself
Most of us have difficulty accepting others because we have difficulty accepting ourselves. We know our personal insecurities, hidden guilt, and imperfections, both large and small. Secretly, we believe that we don't measure up, no matter what others say and think. In short, we have difficulty accepting ourselves because we haven't consciously given ourselves permission to not be perfect.

In order to accept the faults and shortcomings of others, we must first come to terms with our own faults and shortcomings. If we haven't given ourselves permission to be human—to be not perfect—how can we begin to give others that same permission? As you give the gift of acceptance to others, you'll be required to become more accepting of yourself as well. This self-acceptance will force you to become gentler on yourself, and that might be one of the most loving things you do for yourself.

Learn to Float Again
If you're like me, you learned to swim. (And if you didn't, keep reading. This might just inspire you to sign up for those swim lessons.) Before we learned to propel ourselves through the water, we had to learn to float—to lie on our backs, let our legs and arms dangle, and just relax and do nothing.

This act of letting go, of simply floating, is one of the most difficult skills swimming requires. It's difficult because it involves trust—trust that the water will hold us up, trust that our lungs will provide the needed bouyancy, and trust that we won't drown. We tend to tighten up, move our arms, and kick our legs. But once we let go, we're rewarded with the realization that we can keep our heads above water without very much effort.

Accepting others is just like floating. It requires that we do nothing but be present, keep silent, and remain open. The nonverbal and verbal responses of acceptance require that you learn to float again, to let go and trust. Like floating, acceptance requires us to let go of seeing only one way of being and to trust the process of allowing another person to unfold before us. If you do this, you may experience something much more rewarding than swimming.

Don't Accept Unacceptable Behavior
Acceptance has boundaries and limits. To accept a person whose opinions and behaviors are different from your own is a gift that will bring you closer to those you love. However, you need to be alert to any behaviors or situations that could be harmful or dangerous. If you realize that someone's actions are illegal, dangerous, or unacceptable, you need to exercise judgement and do what you feel is necessary to protect yourself and others from physical, emotional, or psychological harm. To be accepting of physical abuse, psychological manipulation, or verbal assault is not only dangerous, but often encourages the escalation of such behavior. Know your boundaries of acceptable and unacceptable behaviors.

Express Your Thoughts and Feelings, Too
The purpose of accepting others is not to transform you into a wishy-washy person with no opinions or feelings. Quite the contrary, the purpose is to enable you to create open, supportive relationships wherein the expression of opinions and emotions can be freely shared by both you and your loved ones. By being accepting of different opinions and behaviors, you are setting the stage for open and tolerant relationships in your life that have the freedom to develop and grow. But remember to express your thoughts and feelings along the way.

Acceptance is the basis of all relationships. Whether it's a romantic partner, family member, or friend, acceptance provides the foundation on which individuals in the relationship are free to experience one another more openly. Your decision to give the gift of acceptance will dramatically change all your relationships.

∽

3.1 Personal Exploration: Finger Follow Exercise

This exploration will teach your body (not your mind) how to follow or accept other people. You'll need another person to complete this exercise.

You and your partner sit comfortably in chairs facing each other, close enough so your knees can touch. Your partner raises the index finger of her right hand to about eye level and points in your direction. You raise the index finger of your left hand so it is within one or two inches of her finger. Pretend a sheet of glass extends from the floor to above your heads, separating you and your partner.

For three minutes, your partner moves her finger in the two-dimensional space that separates you. The object is to follow your partner's finger with yours. No matter where your partner moves her finger, you follow it as best you can. Your partner is not to move her finger so quickly that it's impossible for you to follow. And neither of you is allowed to talk for the three minutes. Just see what it's like to accept what is and follow her finger.

Briefly describe your response to this exercise.

_____

_____

_____

3.2 Practice Giving: Accepting a Loved One

Select one person with whom you are in a relationship. Identify one minor belief, behavior, or habit this individual has that you have difficulty accepting (nothing major or extreme). Your gift to this person is to demonstrate acceptance of this belief, behavior, or habit during the next week. Identify two specific verbal or nonverbal ways you will give this gift of acceptance.

Name of the individual: _____

Belief, behavior, or habit: _____

List two verbal or nonverbal ways to give the gift of acceptance.

1. _____

2. _____

Date by which you will give this gift: _____

3.3   Practice Giving: Accepting Yourself

Identify one minor belief, behavior, or habit you have difficulty accepting in yourself (nothing major or extreme). Your gift to yourself is to simply accept the fact that you have this belief, behavior, or habit for one week without feeling guilty. Whenever the urge arises to evaluate or blame yourself, immediately tell yourself, "It's okay. I've given myself permission to accept my shortcoming for one week." This might be the nicest gift you give yourself this week.

Belief, behavior, or habit: _____

Do you agree to give yourself permission to accept this belief, behavior, or habit for one week without evaluating or blaming yourself? ___ I do. (You get only one choice. Be nice to yourself!)

Listening for Understanding

"The first duty of love is to listen."
—Eric Fromm

From where I was sitting, I could see the branches of the oak tree bending over the brook just outside my office window. The afternoon shadows were growing long against the autumn leaves on the banks of the creek as my mind returned to the two people seated in front of me. Gary and Rachael were my last appointment of the day. This was their second marriage counseling session and Gary was practicing his new paraphrasing skills with Rachael.

"I need you to pay more attention to me," Rachael said, holding the pencil in her hand that signified it was her turn to be heard. When she felt Gary understood her statement by his paraphrasing, she would hand the pencil to him and he would take a turn at speaking.

"Are you saying you want me home from work earlier?" asked Gary.

"No, that's not what I mean. I want you to talk to me more," she clarified.

"But I do talk to you, all the time!" he quickly shot back.

"No," I interrupted. "You're not to defend yourself, Gary. Your only goal is to understand Rachael's statement. Now try again."

"Okay, okay," he moaned. "Do you mean, Rachael, you want you and me to have more conversations when I am home?"

"Yes, that's what I mean!" she beamed and handed the pencil to Gary.

"This listening stuff isn't easy." Gary said as he took the pencil.

Real listening isn't ever easy. In fact, listening is one of the most difficult yet essential gifts you need to give in any relationship. Whether you're responding to the statements of a new friend or attempting to improve a twenty-year relationship, listening plays a vital role.

Your willingness and ability to suspend your own needs and desires for a period of time and focus solely on the speaker is one of the basic building blocks of relational communication. How can we build those connections, those bridges to loved ones, without setting aside our thoughts and feelings while focusing on what they're communicating?

A body of research in communication and counseling suggests that we each spend approximately half of our waking lives listening to others, while the other half involves speaking, reading, writing, and other forms of communication. Half of our lives listening! And yet, how many of us truly know how to listen?

Very few in fact, judging from the complaints of hundreds of clients in counseling and students in my college courses. The majority of them complain that their loved ones don't really listen. Not many of us have received training in the skill of listening.

The purpose of listening is to accurately receive the intended message of the speaker. Recall that the meaning of a message is in people and not in the words. This listening process is achieved through a series of negotiations between the speaker and the listener in a communication setting.

In the story, the word "attention" for Rachael meant her wish for more interaction with Gary. In her mind's eye she was envisioning more conversations with her husband. For Gary, the word "attention" meant increased time spent at home with his wife. In his mind's eye he saw himself having to come home earlier and not spending as much time with his buddies after work.

But as Gary tried to really "see" what his wife was "seeing" by **paraphrasing,** or reflecting the content of her words, he was able to get a more accurate picture of what she intended. They had negotiated for meaning. Their efforts, back and forth, to clarify and reflect the content of Rachael's message, proved successful. Gary demonstrated that he had indeed understood what she was saying. He had given his wife the gift of listening for understanding.

POOR LISTENING STYLES

Much of what passes for listening in relationships is not really listening at all but rather behaviors that prevent true communication. Many of our behaviors give the impression we are listening when in fact we are day-dreaming, arranging rebuttals, or changing the subject to accommodate our interests.

Here are four styles of listening to avoid when a loved one talks with you: refusing to listening, pretending to listen, listening selectively, and listening to evaluate.

Refusing to Listen

The most obvious listening style that prevents understanding is no listening at all—when you refuse to listen to someone else's statements. This is not necessarily a bad or inappropriate communication strategy, especially when you are communicating your conscious decision to end a relationship, terminate a discussion, or protect yourself from insult or injury. But remember that your refusal to listen can hurt the relationship. Here are some examples of refusing to listen:

simply walking away when someone begins speaking
I don't want to talk about this issue any more.
No, I don't want to hear what you have to say.
Shut up.

Pretending to Listen

The second style of listening that prevents understanding is pretending to listen. In this style, the listener demonstrates many of the nonverbal behaviors of true listening—open posture, eye contact, nodding, and appropriate facial expressions—but makes no attempt to receive and process the content of the speaker's message. Here are some examples of this listening style:

Yes, dear.
Yeah, I hear you already.
Okay, I got the message.
Whatever.

Listening Selectively

In the third style of listening that prevents understanding, the listener attends and responds to only those subjects of personal interest. In other words, the listener listens selectively, not to the entire message. We've all endured the individual who listens to us just long enough to bring up a topic he's interested in and then dominates the conversation. Here are some examples of selective listening:

Yeah, I'm glad you brought that up because I had that happen to me.
Well, now you're talking about something I'm interested in.
That reminds me of a time when I...
Yeah, but what happened to me was...

Listening to Evaluate

Listening to evaluate is the most common listening style we use. Listening to evaluate focuses on judging the correctness, rightness, or worth of the speaker's statements. Rather than hearing and trying to understand the speaker's opinions, feelings, and frame of reference, the listener is concerned about judging the message from his or her own point of view.

It doesn't matter whether the listener's evaluation is negative or positive; the purpose of listening is to judge the speaker. Whether the listener's response is "That's a wonderful point and I agree wholeheartedly with it!" or "That's the most ridiculous opinion I've ever heard!" the deeper message is "I am the judge of your comments." Listening for the purpose of judging does not encourage or provide a basis of understanding. Here are some examples of listening to evaluate:

No, I disagree.
That's a good point.
You're wrong.
How can you say that?

There are some occasions when using one of these four styles of listening will be appropriate. But when your primary purpose for listening is to connect with a loved one, then you should avoid these four styles.

How then, should we listen? The best way to listen for understanding in relationships is by active listening.

ACTIVE LISTENING FOR UNDERSTANDING

Traditionally, listening has been viewed as a passive activity. The speaker talks. The listener hears. The speaker is active and verbal and the listener is passive and silent. When the speaker finishes talking, the assumption is that the message has been accurately received by the listener, with no observable effort or participation on the listener's part. What could be simpler? The speaker talks and the listener listens. But listening demands the active participation of the listener.

We use active listening to make sure that the message the listener receives is the message the speaker intended. **Active listening** is the process in which the listener tells the speaker what her message means to him. It enables the listener to prove to the speaker that the message she sent was accurately received. And it also gives the speaker the opportunity to confirm the listener's interpretations or clarify them when incorrect. True communication requires the active participation of the listener, as well as the speaker.

There are two types of active listening: active listening for content (accuracy) and active listening for feelings (empathy). In fact, all communication occurs on these two levels. The **content level** deals with the intellectual subject of a conversation, which includes such things as your thoughts, plans, values, decisions, or the price of food at a restaurant. In contrast, the **feeling level** deals with your emotional responses to a conversation—the world of love and hate, pleasure and pain. How do you feel about your thoughts, plans, values, decisions, or the price of food at a restaurant?

The content level of communication involves the head. The feeling level involves the heart. These two levels of communication coexist and exert their influence on each other. Let's examine how you can actively listen for the content and feelings of what your loved one is communicating to you.

Active Listening: A Four-Step Process

The basic steps in the active listening process are the same for both content and feelings. If you follow these four simple steps in communicating with others, you will have mastered one of the fundamental skills of effective communication—listening for understanding.

Step 1: Speaker makes a statement.

Step 2: Listener paraphrases speaker's statement. ("Are you saying...?")

Step 3: Speaker accepts paraphrase ("Yes, that's what I meant") or rejects paraphrase ("No, that's not what I meant")

Step 4: If rejected, speaker repeats Step 1 to clarify original statement. If accepted, listener is free to express thought/feeling.

Here is an example of active listening for content (accuracy):

Rachael: I need you to pay more attention to me.
Gary: **Are you saying** you want us to have more conversations?
Rachael: That's exactly what I mean!

Here is an example of active listening for feeling (empathy):

Tim: I don't think I'll have a job after the next downsizing at work.
Jillian: **Are you feeling** worried about being fired?
Tim: Yeah, I don't know what I'll do if I lose my job.
Jillian: **You're feeling** lost if you had to look for work?
Tim: You got it. I just wouldn't know where to begin.

Did you notice how, in both examples, the listeners actively reflected what they thought they had heard from the speakers by saying, "Are you saying...?" and "Are you feeling...?" An easy way to remember the essence of active listening is to think of yourself as a mirror reflecting the content or feeling of the message back to the speaker. In the next two dialogues, the first paraphrase is incorrect. The listeners and speakers negotiate for understanding using Steps 3 and 4 of the active listening process.

Dad: I want us to be closer this coming year.
Joie: **Are you saying** I have to visit home more?
Dad: No. I'd enjoy talking with you more—about your future and stuff.
Joie: **You mean** you want to know how I'm feeling about life?
Dad: I'd love that! We don't seem to talk like we used to since you moved into your own apartment.
Joie: That would be fun for me too, Dad.

Sonya: I want to sign up for more courses next semester even though my grades aren't too high this semester.

Roy: **Are you feeling** hopeful about getting better grades next semester?

Sonya: No. The grades aren't important to me. I just like going to college.

Roy: So **you're feeling** excited about just attending college?

Sonya: Yes! I really like learning about new things. I feel like I have all sorts of opportunities available.

Did you notice how the listeners and the speakers had to repeat the process one more time to get the message or feeling communicated accurately? This simple technique of actively reflecting the content of the message back to the speaker is effective in assuring the accurate reception of the thought or idea sent by the speaker. Next we'll explore some variations of the active listening process.

ACTIVE LISTENING FOR CONTENT

Here are three variations of the active listening process for testing the accuracy of the content sent by the speaker—you questions, active listening questions, and active listening statements.

You Questions

The most basic form of active listening is mirroring back to the speaker the content of the message with a question beginning with the word "You…." Here are some examples of you questions:

Jerry: My babysitter is sick and I'm stuck again.

Ariah: **You** don't know who's going to watch your children?

Jerry: Yeah.

Ned: I think I need to look again at the cost of graduate school.

Elena: So **you** think tuition and books might be too expensive for us?

Ned: Yes. But also I don't know if I want to devote all that time to studying.

Active Listening Questions

The second type of active listening involves asking the speaker if what you heard is correct by beginning your interpretation of the speaker's statement with such statements as "Do you mean...?" "Are you saying...?" and"Do I understand you to say...?"Here are some examples of active listening questions:

Ted: Being in a serious relationship is more work that I thought.
Polly: **Are you saying** it demands a lot of your time?
Ted: No, my partner just wants to talk and I'm not a talker.

Juan: My kids have changed since I've left.
Gil: **Do you mean** they're different since you and Mia separated?
Juan: Yeah. They don't talk or pay attention to me.

Active Listening Statements

The third way you can reflect the content of the speaker's message is by using statements that introduce your interpretation:"I hear you saying...," "What you're saying...," "I understand you to mean...," and "It sounds like you...." Here are some examples of active listening statements:

It sounds like you want to quit your job.
I hear you saying that you wish we'd spend more money on vacations.
What you're saying is you don't want to see my folks this weekend.

All three active listening techniques for content will help you clearly and accurately understand the thoughts and ideas your loved one is trying to share with you. These techniques will enable you to make certain that the pictures you construct in your mind's eye are the same as the ones your loved one is attempting to communicate. Let's use active listening to check our understanding of our loved one's feelings.

ACTIVE LISTENING FOR FEELINGS

Many misunderstandings, arguments, and conflicts at the content level in a relationship are due to feeling level issues. Oftentimes people need to share and vent emotions before they can begin solving problems or resolving conflict. If you can listen for feelings, especially during conflict or emotionally charged discussions, you can encourage their expression and exploration. The communication of feelings is essential in understanding your loved ones.

The following are five ways you can listen for feelings when communicating with your loved ones: observe the speaker's nonverbal communication; reflect the speaker's nonverbal behavior; reflect the speaker's feelings; respond to the speaker's verbal communication, and listen to your intuition.

Observe the Speaker's Nonverbal Communication

You can listen to the feelings of someone you love not only with your ears but also with your eyes. The nonverbal cues communicated by the speaker, either consciously or unconsciously, constantly bombard your senses during a conversation. A person's posture, physical position relative to you, facial expressions, eye contact, gestures, tone of voice, rate of speech, breathing pattern, and touching behavior are just a few of the numerous nonverbal cues that communicate messages to you.

The next time you are talking with a loved one, pretend that you cannot hear him and instead focus on the nonverbal behaviors. Don't tune the person out completely. Remain in the conversation, but focus half your attention on what the nonverbal behaviors are communicating to you. Anything you observe during the discussion is communicating that person's feelings and emotions.

By paying more attention to the nonverbal communication of others you will be more effective in describing their behaviors and reflecting their feelings. Give the gift of listening for feelings, with your eyes!

Reflect the Speaker's Nonverbal Behavior

We are often so unaware of our feelings in this culture that many times we are blind to the emotions are bodies are communicating to others. I think we're all guilty of this more than we'd care to admit. You can listen to the feelings of loved ones by making them consciously aware of their unconscious nonverbal messages. Often an individual is unaware of a downcast eye, a raised voice, an increase in breathing rate, a reddening of the face, or the relaxation of a frown. Many times these nonverbal behaviors go unnoticed by both speaker and listener.

If, however, you notice a nonverbal behavior that you believe is communicating an emotional message worth mentioning, you could simply share your perception, without any value judgment associated with it. Rather than state, "It looks like you're getting scared and frightened," you might say, "I notice that you keep looking at the window and your breathing is getting faster." This statement could invite the individual to talk about his feelings. Here are some phrases you might want to use when you listen for feelings:

I notice that you're not looking at me now.
I see that you're looking at the clock.
I hear you sigh when I...
I'm seeing that you frown when I talk about...
I notice that you're smiling when I talk about...

Reflect the Speaker's Feelings

Often people will be aware of a feeling they are experiencing, but are reluctant to share or communicate that emotion with you. Yet during the course of the conversation, their emotional responses to the content of the discussion or to you personally become more apparent to you as you observe their nonverbal behaviors. A reddening of the face, a tightening of the neck, shallowness of the breathing, an increased rate of speech or volume, a withdrawing of position or posture, folded arms, or diverted eye contact can communicate their feelings. At such a moment, you might decide to listen for feelings by reflecting the emotion or emotions you think they are experiencing. Here are some phrases that will introduce your feeling reflection:

Are you feeling/experiencing...?
It seems like you're feeling...?
Is this discussion making you feel...?
Am I making you feel...?
You look like you're feeling...?

Respond to the Speaker's Verbal Communication

There are two instances when the speaker will verbally invite you to communicate at the feeling level of communication. First, when the speaker shares a feeling statement with you, and second, when the speaker asks you how you're feeling. In each case, you can shift the conversation from content level communication to feeling level communication. In the first instance, the speaker will share a feeling statement with you, such as "I'm feeling happy," "I'm feeling upset," or "This situation makes me feel discouraged." Be sensitive to such feeling statements, and respond to them by reflecting the speaker's feeling statement with a paraphrase that encourages the speaker to comment further or explore the feeling. Here are some examples:

> I'm feeling happy.
> So, you're feeling pretty pleased?
>
> I'm feeling upset.
> Are you feeling distressed?
>
> This situation makes me feel discouraged.
> Sounds like you're feeling defeated?

The purpose of paraphrasing, or reflecting a feeling statement, is to prove to the speaker that you have received the message and to encourage the speaker to remain at the feeling level by exploring or expanding on his statement.

The second way you can listen for feelings is to respond to the speaker's specific invitations to communicate at the feeling level. When the speaker asks you how you're feeling about a particular issue, person, or situation, you can respond with an appropriate feeling response instead of remaining at the content level. Here are some examples:

> Are you angry with your father's decision?
> Yes, I am upset with Dad.
>
> Does this situation make you feel secure?
> No, I'm still feeling insecure and vulnerable.
>
> Am I making you feel comfortable?
> Yes, I'm not feeling nervous or frightened.

Responding to the speaker's feeling statement or invitation for you to share feelings is a way of joining in the communication of feelings. You are listening to the feelings of others. Instead of changing the subject and diverting the conversation back to the content level, you accept the invitation to shift the discussion to the feeling level of communication.

Listen to Your Intuition

There are times when a speaker's nonverbal and verbal communication do not communicate any emotional disturbance or conflict, but you have a nagging suspicion that something is wrong. You can't seem to put your finger on the exact reason for your uneasiness, but your intuition tells you that something is not right. If this feeling continues, you might want to listen to your intuition and share your hunch with your loved one.

Often, our unconscious mind is sensitive to and aware of emotional messages that radiate from the speaker, which could be different from the verbal and nonverbal communication. Perhaps it is the language of the soul or spirit that is the source of this yet-to-be-discovered form of communication. Whatever the reason, you might want to share your intuition with the speaker. Here are some examples of such statements:

It's nothing you've said or done, but I have a feeling you're upset.
My intuition is telling me that something isn't right. Are you mad?
My spirit is telling me that you're feeling distrustful. Is that so?

This final way of listening for feelings might not sound logical or reasonable. If it doesn't work for you, don't use it. My reason for suggesting it is that occasionally my intuition senses things in counseling and in my personal life that neither verbal nor nonverbal channels of communication provide. It's difficult to put into words, but you might want to be open to that small voice deep inside you when listening for feelings.

FEELING LANGUAGE

Without a vocabulary for this feeling level of communication, discussion is rather limited and difficult. In my relationship classes, I have all my students take an informal feeling vocabulary test to demonstrate our limited language of emotions. On a blank sheet of paper I have each student list as many feeling words as he or she can in two minutes. The results are rather startling. Men will usually list eight to ten feeling words in two minutes. Words like good, bad, happy, and mad are among the usual responses. Women, on the other hand, will list between twenty and thirty words during the same period of time. These results show that women have conscious command of at least twice as many feeling words as men.

The implications of these results are compelling, especially in light of the **Sapir–Worf Hypothesis,** which suggests that a person's language not only reports reality, but also acts to structure our perceptions of reality. In other words, language can act like windows that allow us to see the world outside. If we have one or two windows, our view of reality or the outside world is limited. On the other hand, if we have a hundred windows, our view of reality is much more expansive and inclusive. The more words, the more reality experienced.

People with a limited feeling vocabulary usually experience a limited emotional world. An extreme example is someone who possesses only two feeling words in his vocabulary—good and bad. His description of all his emotional life experiences would be confined to "good" or "bad." The death of his friend and stubbing his toe would both be described as events that made him feel "bad," whereas love for his child and his enjoyment in eating candy would both be described as "good." What a life.

Whether the Sapir-Worf Hypothesis is true or not, I believe that everyone should have an array of feeling words at their command. Not only can we enlarge the number of ways to describe our emotional experience, but more important, we might also expand our awareness of what there is to experience at the feeling level. The following list will help increase your feeling vocabulary:

accepted	edgy	intense	restless
afraid	elated	intimidated	sad
annoyed	embarrassed	irritable	sensual
anxious	enthusiastic	jazzed	sentimental
ashamed	ecstatic	joyful	shaky
bashful	excited	lonely	shy
bewildered	fearful	moving	silly
bitter	foolish	mean	strong
bored	free	miserable	subdued

brave	frustrated	needed	tender
calm	furious	neglected	tense
confident	glum	nervous	terrified
confused	guilty	peaceful	tired
defeated	happy	pessimistic	trapped
defensive	helpless	playful	ugly
depressed	high	pleased	uneasy
detached	hopeful	pressured	uptight
disappointed	hostile	protective	vulnerable
disgusted	humiliated	puzzled	warm
disturbed	hurt	rejected	weak
eager	inadequate	relieved	worried

Have fun incorporating these words into your daily language. Make a copy of this list and share it with a loved one. Hang a copy of this list on the refrigerator or the bathroom mirror. One client of mine taped his list to the dashboard of his pickup. You'll discover that the more you study and use these words, the more aware of your emotional life you will become.

GUIDELINES FOR LISTENING

There are no hard and fast rules for listening for the thoughts and feelings of others, but you might find these five guidelines helpful: decide to listen, avoid judging, refrain from giving advice, focus on the speaker's thoughts and feelings, and remember that listening can change a person.

Decide to Listen
Your decision to listen to others is not itself a feeling. It is a conscious, intellectual choice to focus on your loved ones. You may not feel good about what is said, but it is your conscious decision to be open to the thoughts and feelings of another so a deeper relationship can be established and maintained.

Avoid Judging
After you have decided to give the gift of listening for understanding, refrain from judging the speaker's thoughts and feelings. This is your gift to the speaker, remember? You are the listener who is attempting to under-

stand and empathize with the speaker's feelings, not yours. This gift is not about you. This is not about how you're feeling and what you're thinking. It's about the other person—the person you love. No matter what the speaker shares, your duty is to demonstrate understanding. Later in the conversation you may want share your thoughts and feelings, but not now. Now is the time to simply give the gift of listening for feelings.

Refrain from Giving Advice

Also refrain from giving advice or any other form of guiding or directing. Even though you believe your advice would be helpful, don't give advice during this phase of the conversation. This is your time to give the gift of listening, not talking. You can give your advice later. For now, your job— your gift—is to listen for the speaker's thoughts and feelings.

Focus on the Speaker's Thoughts and Feelings

Whether this process takes one minute, fifteen minutes, or an hour, put aside your own responses for a period of time and listen for the speaker's thoughts and feelings. Detach from your ego—your desire to defend, evaluate, advise, fix, solve, or attack—and focus on the speaker. Like a counselor, your duty is to listen to the speaker.

Remember That Listening Can Change a Person

Keep in mind that your gift of listening can change your loved one. Just the fact that you remain silent for a time and focus your attention on your loved one, not on your own wants and needs, can be enough to change how she thinks and feels. Your loved one will feel important, valued, and attended to by your simple gift of listening and this will affect how she sees and feels about you. Many a relationship has been greatly improved by listening.

Listening for understanding may be one of the most precious gifts you can give. It can bring understanding, appreciation, and healing to any relationship. This gift begins with your decision to remain silent and listen to the thoughts and feelings of your loved ones. How else will you ever know their true thoughts and feelings? Give the gift of listening for understanding.

4.1 Personal Exploration: Watching Silent Television

To increase your awareness and sensitivity of nonverbal communication behaviors, watch a half-hour television sitcom without sound. Mute the volume and observe the nonverbal behaviors of the actors. Can you figure out the main story line by simply watching the nonverbal behaviors without sound? Were you more aware of the actors' movement and behaviors than you usually are when you can hear their voices and listen to the background sounds and music? Try to use this new awareness and sensitivity the next time you talk with a loved one.

What was this experience like for you?

_____

_____

_____

_____

4.2 Practice Giving: Pencil Technique

Practice active listening with a loved one. First explain the four-step active listening process to your partner. Then your partner, holding a pencil to signify that he or she is the speaker, makes a statement about something he or she needs from you. Paraphrase your partner's message. When your partner is satisfied with your paraphrase, then you take the pencil and make a statement about something you need from your partner. Finally, your partner paraphrases your message to your satisfaction.

How did you and your partner do with active listening?

_____

_____

_____

_____

4.3 Practice Giving: Active Listening for Feelings

In your next conversation with a loved one, be aware of any non-verbal behaviors or verbal comments that suggest a desire to communicate at the feeling level. Decide to listen for feelings. Use active listening for feelings and attempt to communicate at the feeling level with your loved one. Try to keep the conversation at the feeling level for two or three minutes.

How did it feel to listen for feelings?

_____

_____

_____

Did you notice any differences in your communication?

_____

_____

_____

_____

Asking Questions

～

"Your questions reveal your heart."
–Voltaire

The giant expanse of the Canadian plains stretched before of us, like a vast ocean revealing the curvature of the earth. Our boys were asleep in the back seat of the car as I followed this nameless two-lane road in southern Saskatchewan on a warm July afternoon. There wasn't a house to be seen in this rolling sea of wheat fields far from our home in the coastal foothills of California. My wife's eyes were beginning to close as I listened to the dull hum of the tires on the pavement.

Vicky wasn't asleep because I heard her ask, "What are you thinking about? You look worried."

"No," I smiled.

"But you look worried," she repeated.

"Well, maybe. I guess I'm still thinking about the argument with Tom," I admitted.

Tom is a colleague of mine at the college where I teach. Before leaving for summer vacation, Tom and I had a disagreement about a departmental policy. We both said some strong words, and I was still troubled by the incident.

"Still upset?" Vicky asked.

"Yeah. I feel uncomfortable having to see him in the fall."

"Oh, I see. Just wouldn't know what to say?"

"I hope he apologizes. Then it'd be okay."

"And if he doesn't?" Vicky inquired.

"Well, I could invite him to lunch before classes start or maybe just leave him a phone message."

"Anything else?"

"I thought about dropping him and Fran a postcard from Winnipeg."

"Sounds like you've given this some thought. Which do you like best?"

"The postcard. I can at least apologize for my small part of the argument." I smiled.

Four days later, I sent Tom and Fran a postcard from Winnipeg. It had a beautiful picture of the vast plains of Canada.

⌒

Before Vicky and I were married, we attended four premarital counseling sessions. I don't remember much of what was said during those four hours, but I do recall one remark the counselor directed to me.

"Your partner should provide you with good counsel," she said.

"Does that mean Vicky should always know what to do?" I asked.

"No," she replied. "Your wife should let you solve your own problems. Her counsel, like yours, should provide clarity and encouragement for you to see your own solutions. The best way to achieve this is by asking questions and not by giving your own solutions. You'll need to develop the art of asking one another questions."

When you give the gift of asking questions of loved ones, you are focusing your attention on them, not on you. You provide an invitation for them to open up, to share, and ultimately to connect with you.

Your questions can provide a safe place for them to see themselves, to help them explore and examine their own thoughts and feelings, not merely reflect them as you do when you actively listen for content or feelings. Your questions can help them acknowledge, explore, and solve their own problems. Asking questions of a loved one can be a helpful and enlightening gift, if you ask the right questions.

ASKING THE RIGHT QUESTIONS

Asking the right kinds of questions is vital to encouraging dialogue and connection in love relationships. Questions can direct, evoke, and encourage the speaker to clarify, focus, and explore. Let's look at four categories of questions—closed, open, probing, and loaded.

Closed Questions

Closed questions can be answered in a word or two. They don't really encourage the speaker to develop, expand, or explore the topic. Instead, they focus, limit, and highlight. Here are some examples of closed questions and possible answers:

> Do you feel excited?   yes/no/maybe
> Were you thinking about calling him?   yes/no/maybe
> Are you right or wrong?   right/wrong
> Did she talk to him pleasantly?   yes/no/none of your business
> Do you mean you want to stay in the relationship?   yes/no/maybe

Closed questions require the speaker to focus attention on a specific inquiry and respond briefly. The purpose of closed questions is not to develop and explore, but rather to focus and specify.

Open Questions

Unlike closed questions, open questions encourage the speaker to develop, expand, and explore a topic in greater detail and depth. Open questions usually begin with the words "Why," "What," and "How," or contain the words "Explain" and "Describe" within them. Here are some examples of open questions:

> Why are you excited?
> Why were you thinking about calling him?
> What makes you feel you're right in this matter?
> How did she talk to him?
> Can you explain your reasons for wanting to stay in the relationship?

Notice that these open questions correspond to the closed questions above. Do you see how the reworded open questions encourage more depth and detail from the speaker than do the closed questions?

Both open and closed questions are useful to help a loved one solve a problem.

Probing Questions

After the speaker begins to explore a topic, you can assist her by asking probing questions. Probing questions are open and closed questions that are directly related to the preceding statement in a conversation. The aim of probing questions is to further encourage the speaker to explain, expand, and develop a thought, idea, or feeling.

Remember that probing questions are intended for the benefit of the speaker's examination and development of a topic, not for your own curiosity or personal interest. Notice in the beginning story how my wife asked many closed and open probing questions that helped me examine my predicament with my colleague. Here are two brief dialogues to help you get the feel of open and closed probing questions:

Tia: I think we should do something special for our anniversary.
Greg: Like what, honey? (open probe)
Tia: We could go to a nice restaurant.
Greg: What kind of food would you like? (open probe)

Bart: I'm not feeling good about my life.
Cara: What part of your life? (open probe)
Bart: Oh, my job.
Cara: How is your job not meeting your expectations? (open probe)
Bart: I haven't advanced like I thought I would. I thought I'd be in management by now.
Cara: So promotions haven't come as you expected? (closed probe)
Bart: Yeah. I'm always passed by when there's a management opening.
Cara: What do you want to do about this? (open probe)

Did you notice in the second example how Cara didn't evaluate or give advice? Instead, she asked open and closed probing questions to help Bart express his problem more specifically and then led the discussion to possible solutions. Imagine how this conversation would have gone if Cara had responded differently in the beginning.

Bart: I'm not feeling good about my life.
Cara: Quit feeling sorry for yourself.

What a difference one sentence can make. Instead of saying "Quit feeling sorry for yourself," Cara chose to ask questions that helped Bart express his thoughts and feelings. Just like Cara, your decision to give the gift of asking questions can make all the difference in a conversation, and in the relationship.

Loaded Questions

Loaded questions contain accusations. Although they are structured like questions, often their real intent is to accuse, blame, and judge. They also indirectly force your own opinion and advice on the listener. Here are some examples of loaded questions:

Do you still criticize your sister?
Does he agree with everything she says?
Are you always disgusted with everything I do?
Are you going to ace this test like all the rest?
How long will this relationship last?

Avoid asking loaded questions in your communication with loved ones. If you want to discuss issues that are bothering you with a loved one, you need to be more direct and gentle about raising such topics.

THE HELPS METHOD: QUESTIONS THAT DISCOVER SOLUTIONS

Now let's look at a specific method in which you use questioning to help your loved ones explore and find a solution to a problem. This method builds on the gift of listening to others, and adds three more skills—exploring a problem, brainstorming solutions, and selecting a solution. The steps for accomplishing these skills are summarized in the acronym HELPS:

H ONOR the speaker's thoughts and feelings.

E XPLORE the speaker's problem.

L IST possible solutions.

P ROPOSE a solution.

S TART the solution.

Step 1: HONOR the Speaker's Thoughts and Feelings

The first step is to accept the speaker's thoughts and feelings about the issue or problem she is sharing with you. Just like active listening, you withhold evaluation and judgment. You refrain from fixing, solving, advising, punishing, blaming, accusing, directing, teaching, and so forth. Your first step is to honor or accept the speaker's thoughts and feelings without trying to judge or change. As psychiatrist and author Carl Jung wisely observed, "Nothing can be changed or improved without first accepting it."

Step 2: EXPLORE the Speaker's Problem

The second step is to help the speaker explore her problem. Before the speaker can arrive at a solution, she needs to examine the problem.

Most people don't even know where to begin. Often their response is to blame or attack rather than to explore the nature of the problem. You can assist the speaker by asking questions about the problem. Here's a list of suggested questions you might want to ask the speaker:

1. What is the problem?
2. How serious is the problem?
3. Whom does the problem affect?
4. How long has this problem affected you?
5. What are the causes of the problem?
6. What actions or solutions have you attempted?
7. What will happen if this problem is not solved?
8. Do you want to invest energy and effort into solving this problem?

Don't feel you have to ask all of these questions or in any specific order. The important thing is that your questions keep the speaker focused on exploring and examining the problem.

Remember to ask probing questions that enable the speaker to develop and gain insight into the problem. Don't get sidetracked by asking questions to satisfy your curiosity. This is the gift of asking questions for the benefit of your loved one.

Step 3: LIST Possible Solutions

After the problem has been explored to the satisfaction of the speaker, you can have your loved one **brainstorm** or generate a list of possible solutions to the problem. This is not an easy process, because the speaker will initially resist your suggestion that there are any solutions to this obviously hopeless situation. But don't be discouraged. Be positive, encouraging, and gentle. Here are four hints that will help you in your efforts:

1. **No evaluation.** Do not evaluate or let your loved one evaluate any solution. This goes against our natural inclination to immediately critique every solution that comes to mind. "No, that won't work," "No, that's too expensive," and "No, that's silly" are just a few common evaluations.
2. **Keep a list of the solutions.** You should take notes as the speaker generates ideas. This way, the speaker can focus on thinking of possible solutions rather than looking at the ones she has come up with.
3. **Encourage quantity.** The goal is for the speaker to propose as many solutions as possible. Quantity, not quality (at least not yet).
4. **The wilder the better.** Get crazy, be silly, and have fun.

When you have at least fifteen possible solutions, no matter how silly or impossible to implement, summarize the list for the speaker. Combine solutions that can fit together. Add a last solution or two. Now you're ready for the fourth step.

Step 4: PROPOSE a Solution

Review the list of possible solutions with the speaker. Draw a line through the most ridiculous, impractical, and illegal solutions. Circle the remaining solutions. Have the speaker look at the list again and select her top three solutions from the circled list. Then draw a line through the circled solutions she did not select.

During the remainder of the session, have the speaker discuss the strengths and weaknesses of the top three solutions. This is the first time you can have an opinion as you play the role of "devil's advocate." As the devil's advocate, you question and raise objections to any solution the speaker seriously considers. Your questions and objections are intended to test the speaker's reasoning and commitment to each solution.

After extended discussion of the strengths and weaknesses of the top three solutions, the speaker might begin to favor one of them. Ask the speaker if she would be willing to give this particular solution a try. If the answer is no, take a break and then go back to Step 1. If the answer is yes, go to Step 5.

Step 5: START the Solution

In the final step, your loved one begins the solution. Implementing the solution might involve some researching, planning, practicing, and preparing. Take your time as you help the speaker design the implementation of the solution.

After starting the solution, occasionally have the speaker evaluate its effectiveness. Is the solution getting the desired results? How is the speaker feeling about the solution? How are the others involved being affected? If the solution is going well, congratulations! If not, you can modify the solution or return to Step 1 or Step 2 and begin the process again.

No matter what happens, the important thing is that you gave the gift of asking questions to help a loved one solve a problem. You provided the framework within which your loved one was able to explore the problem, generate solutions, decide on a solution, and implement that solution. You didn't solve the problem. You helped your loved one solve the problem. There's a world of difference between these two processes.

GUIDELINES FOR ASKING QUESTIONS

Asking questions is more than just requesting information from a loved one. It communicates your interest in another person. It says you're important to me and I want to know more about you. As you give the gift of asking questions, keep in mind these five guidelines: don't overuse questions, don't use questions to criticize, not all problems have solutions, refer serious issues to professionals, and ask yourself the same questions.

Don't Overuse Questions

A common mistake my students and clients make after learning to use open and closed probing questions is to ask too many questions. They bombard others with more questions than are necessary and quite often the recipient of the questions becomes frustrated or angry. Enough already! Be careful not to overwhelm others with too many questions.

It is the quality of questions, not the quantity of questions, that matters. You're not a reporter, potential employer, or police interrogator. The primary purpose of your questions is to assist your loved ones to clarify, focus, and explore their issues. A few well structured questions will go a long way in helping your loved ones discover what they are really trying to communicate.

Don't Use Questions to Criticize
Be careful not to use questions to blame, accuse, or criticize others. Loaded questions, such as "You really don't love me, do you?" indirectly communicate judgment and tend to initiate or inflame a conflict, not help loved ones explore their problems. Before asking a question, ask yourself, "What is the purpose of my question—to criticize or to help a loved one?" This simple check will help ensure that you enrich a conversation rather than initiate a conflict.

Not All Problems Have Solutions
Don't feel discouraged if your loved one doesn't solve the problem. Not all problems will be resolved satisfactorily. Be prepared for the chance that even with all the assistance you give willingly, your loved one's dilemma will remain. What matters is that your loved one received assistance from you in the face of a problem. You can only do your best at helping your loved one explore a problem and brainstorm solutions. The mere fact that you tried to help is a powerful demonstration of your love and support, regardless of the outcome.

Refer Serious Issues to Professionals
In instances of serious psychological or emotional illness or distress, refer your loved one to a licensed psychiatrist, psychologist, or counselor. Alcohol or chemical addiction, suicidal tendencies, physical abuse, eating disorders, and sexual abuse are examples of issues you are not trained to handle, no matter how well intentioned your efforts. Always refer serious issues to professionals.

Ask Yourself the Same Questions
Occasionally ask yourself the same caring, thought-provoking questions that you pose to your loved ones. Many times we give to others without ever giving to ourselves. The next time you find yourself facing a problem, ask yourself the questions presented in the HELPS Method. You'll

be surprised at how helpful these questions can be when you are the one answering the same questions you often ask.

The gift of asking questions is a very effective way of inviting a loved one to open up, explore, and even solve problems. We've all had the experience of spending time with someone who talked only about themselves and never once asked us a question. This one-sided way of communicating alienates and distances people from one another. By giving the gift of asking questions, your loved ones experience your interest in knowing them, helping them, and connecting with them. By asking the right questions, your loved ones will experience your open heart.

One of the most powerful questions I've ever heard is "How can I love you more?" Ask this question of a loved one and see where the answer takes you. You may discover some new and important things about your loved one as well as yourself. Give the gift of asking questions.

⌒

5.1 **Personal Exploration: Exploring Your Own Problem**

Before you lead someone else through the HELPS Method, you should experience this process yourself. Select one minor personal problem and go through the five steps of the HELPS Method.

What was this process like for you?

_____

_____

_____

5.2 **Practice Giving: Asking Questions of Others**

During the next week, try to ask more open and closed probing questions of your loved ones. Nothing structured or elaborate. Just increase the number of questions you ask those you love. If you're really game, try asking the question we concluded with: "How can I love you more?"

What are some of the interesting, provocative, and helpful questions you used during your conversations with loved ones?

_____

_____

_____

How have these questions influenced or changed your conversations with others?

_____

_____

_____

How have these questions affected you and your relationships?

_____

_____

_____

5.3 Practice Giving: Exploring a Loved One's Problem

When the situation arises, provide the gift of asking questions to help a loved one explore a problem or dilemma. Use the HELPS Method to help him or her find a solution to the problem.

What was this process like for your loved one and you?

_____

_____

_____

_____

Enlarging Others

~

"Every relationship leads you further
into heaven or further into hell."
–Marianne Williamson

*Several years ago I facilitated a support group of nine women, all re-
turning students at our college. We met every Thursday afternoon for
eight weeks during their first semester of school so they could encourage
one another as they became accustomed to college life.*

*During their first session, I asked, "Whom do you go to when you
need encouragement?" Of the nine women in the group, five said they
sought women friends for encouragement, two said their mothers, and
two said their husbands. This surprised me because seven of the nine
women were married.*

*After we discussed this issue for a while, it became apparent few hus-
bands were able or willing to provide the support their wives desired.
Furthermore, many of the women complained their husbands didn't give
any verbal encouragement during this demanding period of their lives.*

*One exception was a tall, dark-haired woman in her early forties who
sat smiling as the other women talked. I turned to her and asked, "Barbara, you shared that your husband is your main source of encouragement. What's he like?"*

*"Well," she began, "Walt's my number one cheerleader. He always
compliments me on the invisible."*

"What do you mean 'the invisible?'" asked one of the women.

"By 'invisible' I mean he compliments me on things I don't do or say. For instance, this morning we were watching the news and there's this story about smoking in restaurants. Walt turns to me and says, 'Barbara, I'm sure glad you don't smoke! And yesterday, we were at Burger King, and a women seated in back of us was swearing at her children. Walt kisses me and whispers, 'I'm glad you don't talk like her.' You see, he compliments me on what I don't do or say, as well as on things I do."

"You mean, you're husband actually compliments you?" asked another woman skeptically.

"Yes he does," Barbara answered. "Being married to him has changed the way I see myself. In fact, he's the reason I'm here. He encouraged me to return to college, now that the kids are in college."

"I wish my husband was like him," sighed one woman.

"Me too," added another.

$$\backsim$$

Barbara's husband, Walt, had an enlarging impact on her. Over the years, his compliments, praise, and encouragement have changed the way she views herself. He enlarged her sense of self. People like Walt have that positive effect on others.

Every time you communicate with people you either enlarge or diminish them by your interaction. Let's say you and I converse for a few minutes. We finally conclude our talk and part company. You could have had two effects on me.

First, you could have diminished me by your words, actions, or attitude. Your overall impact on me could have been negative, even after a minute or two of conversation. As I walk away from you, I could mutter something to myself like, "What a drag he was. I was feeling pretty good until I talked with him." You also could have no conscious impact on me. In other words, I could walk away from our conversation and ask myself, "I wonder what's for lunch?" I consider no impact as a form of negative impact, because I was not enlarged by our interaction at all.

A second and totally different end to this story is that I could have been enlarged by your words, actions, or attitude. Your overall impact on me could have been very positive, even after a few brief moments of conversation. And as I walked away from you, I might have said to myself, "What a wonderful experience. I was feeling a little down before I talked to him, but now life looks a little better."

Two very different results—to enlarge or to diminish someone by our interactions. The example I used was a brief two-minute conversation. Can you imagine the accumulated impact you have on another person over a period of years and after thousands of interactions? It's humbling to think of yourself rubbing off on someone you love over the years. Do you enlarge or diminish others with your words?

WAYS TO ENLARGE OTHERS

Many intangible factors contribute to feeling enlarged by another person. No one particular communication behavior or technique can guarantee that the other person will be enlarged by your interaction with him or her. Therefore, you need to know many ways to enlarge others. Here are five ways you can enlarge others: see and say the best, acknowledge others, compliment others, reframe negatives, and support others.

See and Say the Best
Remember the 80/20 rule? At any given moment, 80 percent of a relationship is working and 20 percent is not. We tend to focus on the 20 percent and neglect the 80 percent. This is the true tragedy of most relationships, I believe, and perhaps of life itself. We're usually concerned with what's not right and wishing we had things we don't already possess. And while we are complaining and seeking, 80 percent of the good things in our relationship, and in our life, go unnoticed and unappreciated.

See the best. We need to put more energy into seeing the 80 percent that is working in all our relationships. The first step in enlarging others is to be willing to take a fresh look at your relationships. Focus on those things you appreciate, like, or admire about your loved ones rather than on those things you disapprove of, reject, or dislike.

One technique I teach my clients and students to help them look for the best in others goes like this. Imagine your loved one will die in one year. The individual does not know this. In fact, you are the only one who is permitted to know this secret. But in one year, you will never be with this person again. How would this change the way you look at her? How would this change the way you talk with him? Listen to her? See him?

The response from the women and men who follow this technique is twofold. First, they immediately comment on how much they would miss their loved one, even if they had been complaining about him or her just before I suggested the "one year to live" scenario. The second response is their desire to verbally communicate their love and appreciation.

Isn't it funny how we can go for days, weeks, and perhaps even years, without verbally sharing how much we appreciate the 80 percent of everything our loved one means to us? We may think these things, but we neglect to share them. Instead, we often talk only about the 20 percent of the relationship we don't like. And sometimes it takes the finality of death to force us even to begin to appreciate those we love.

Say the best. The enlarging impact we have on others begins with our decision to see the best in them. Then we need to be willing to verbally share our appreciation or compliments with them. It is only then that our loved ones become aware of our feelings. Until then, the compliment exists only in our minds. How often we think good things about another, but neglect to share these things with that person.

A teacher I know lives by the motto "If you think it and it's good, share it!" His words strike at what I'm trying to encourage you to do in your attempts to enlarge those you love. If you think it and it's good, share it! Those are indeed wise words to live by. We need to see the 80 percent that is working in every relationship and verbally share it with others.

Acknowledge Others

The easiest way to enlarge loved ones is to notice and acknowledge them. This may sound strange, but I've heard some men and women complain in my classes and in therapy how their loved ones will not even glance up and say hello when they enter the house after being away all day. Now I know this is not the case in all relationships. But there are people who behave as if their loved ones are like silent ghosts who move about the house. We need to acknowledge our loved ones. The two ways to do this are to acknowledge their presence and to acknowledge the relationship.

Acknowledge their presence. The simplest and most basic way to enlarge others is to acknowledge their presence. By that I mean let people know you see them, that you know they're in the same room. Here are some basic statements you can use to acknowledge the presence of a loved one:

Hi! I'm glad to see you!
I was looking forward to seeing you come through the door!
Oh, I didn't know you were out here reading. May I join you?
I'm happy we're home together.

Acknowledge the relationship. Another simple way of enlarging loved ones is to acknowledge their relationship with you. Again, this may sound strange and unnecessary. "Of course my loved ones know I appreciate and value the relationship," we might think. But we need to acknowledge relationships by saying things such as:

How's the love of my life doing today?
I'm happy we're brothers.
You're the best friend I could have ever hoped for.
I'm glad we're a family.

I realize some of these comments may sound obvious or ridiculous, but they are the language of connection. It's worth a try! Who knows, a statement acknowledging your relationship with your loved ones may be just what they need to hear. How will they ever know if you don't tell them?

Compliment Others
One of the most immediate and powerful ways to enlarge loved ones is to compliment them. Yet this is one of the most neglected areas of communication—the art of complimenting another person. We're going to improve that skill by learning to compliment those we love in five specific areas.

Compliment appearance. This is perhaps the easiest form of complimenting behavior. It doesn't require a great deal of experience or skill to say something nice about the appearance of a loved one. You can compliment body, posture, facial expressions, voice, or eyes. Here are a few appearance compliments:

You look radiant.
You have a wonderful smile.
Your voice soothes me.
I like how your eyes shine.

Compliment character. This second form of complimenting requires a little more knowledge of a loved one. It focuses on the internal attractiveness of the person, rather than physical appearance. Such things as kindness, trustworthiness, empathy, loyalty, generosity, optimism, gentleness, humor, and candor are just a few of the thousands of character or personality traits you can compliment. This is a more lasting compliment because these are things that do not diminish with age, such as a nice figure or beautiful hair. Instead, character compliments are directed at the internal nature of your loved one. Here are a few character compliments:

I really appreciate your kindness.
Your optimism makes me feel good.
I like the fact I can trust you with a secret.
Few people have your enthusiasm and zest for life.

Compliment achievement. A third form of complimenting is to compliment achievement. To do this, you simply acknowledge some achievement your loved one has accomplished or realized. The achievement can be as modest as remembering a phone number or as monumental as overcoming some physical disability. Here are some examples of complimenting achievement:

Your photographs are just beautiful.
Congratulations on finishing your English paper!
I'm happy you were elected to the town board.
Good work!

Compliment effort. You can compliment a person even if your loved one doesn't achieve what she or he set out to accomplish. In our culture, we tend to compliment only the winners—those people who finish first and win the awards. But you can compliment your loved ones for the effort they put into an endeavor or project. What matters is that they tried. It's not the destination, but the journey that matters. Here are some examples of complimenting effort:

I'm proud of your efforts.
I'm glad you tried taking this class.

I'm really impressed by the time you invested in your project.
No one else I know puts this much love and effort into a painting.

Compliment the invisible. The fifth and final form of complimenting is
a bit unusual. It involves complimenting your loved ones on the things
they don't do—complimenting the invisible. There are a million things
your loved ones don't do that are worthy of appreciation, yet we rarely
think about those things. Maybe your loved one doesn't swear incessantly,
chain-smoke cigars, or interrupt constantly, so tell him or her.

Once you begin to compliment the invisible, it can become fun and
even entertaining to enlarge your loved one. Here are some examples of
complimenting the invisible:

You could have divorced me, but you chose to stay. I'm glad you did.
I'm grateful you don't overspend on the credit cards.
I'm thankful you don't correct me when we're with friends.
I'm happy you don't watch television all night long.

Reframe Negatives

A creative way of enlarging loved ones is to reframe their negative perception of a situation, circumstance, or person. The reframing technique
involves seeing something from a different perspective or point of view.
We are hurt not so much by what happens, but by our opinion of what
happens. In other words, our perceptions of an event are often more important than the event itself.

How we choose to see something is instrumental in determining how
we will respond to, deal with, and resolve problems that confront us. For
instance, if a loved one is fired from her job nothing can change the fact
she has been fired. But we can view the event from a variety of perspec-
tives. The most obvious perspective is that being fired is a terrible thing.
Your loved one is unemployed and will find another job. How depressing.
Many people would stop here, make no attempt to see this event from a
different point of view, and simply become hurt, angry, or depressed.

But another way of looking at the event is to see it as a new beginning.
For example, your loved one can finally pursue employment more to her
liking. Being fired can be seen as a learning experience. What went wrong?
How can she improve? What skills does she need to develop for future

jobs? Being fired can be viewed as a chance to take a break from the rat race altogether. She can sell everything she owns and hit the road. This one event can be seen in a hundred different ways—no one way more valid than another.

Despite the numerous points of view from which we can choose to see a situation, we tend to get stuck with the first interpretation that pops into our heads. We cement that perspective into our field of vision and limit our emotional responses to that point of view. In short, we're locked into only one way of seeing something.

By reframing, we don't change the person's situation, we simply point out other ways of viewing the same situation. This can have a liberating effect. It releases the individual from the bondage of seeing something from only one point of view. We need to be flexible in our perceptions and interpretations of those events that make up the fabric of our lives.

You can enlarge your loved ones by opening their eyes to other ways of viewing a situation. If they share something "terrible" that has just happened, you can reframe the situation. You can do this by simply stating:

This also could mean…
Another way of looking at this is…
Another interpretation of this is…
You could also see it as…

Your reframe doesn't have to be accepted by the person as the truth, as insightful, or even as a solution to a problem. It's simply a way to avoid getting stuck in only one frame of reference. The reframing technique may help your loved ones feel freer, less confined, and ultimately better able to deal with issues in their lives.

Support Others

A final way to enlarge loved ones is to be on their side rather than be an enemy or adversary. Your goal is to verbally support them in their efforts to grow, improve, or change. Often, supporting your loved ones won't require much more than saying, "I'm on your side." or "I support your decision." But it can also involve giving encouragement, assistance, and motivation over a period of years, even decades. Here are some examples of statements of support:

I support your decision to return to school.
I'm in your corner on this matter.
Let me know how I can help.
I want to support you on this issue.

No matter which way you choose, the important thing is that you are attempting to have an enlarging impact on your loved ones rather than a diminishing one.

I've presented a number of techniques, but don't be concerned or worried that you need to master them all. It just takes one attempt to enlarge a loved one that could make all the difference in the world. Your decision to try to enlarge another person is the most important factor. Don't worry about the small stuff. Just make the decision to enlarge rather than diminish. That's how you give gifts from the heart and communicate for connection with those you love.

GUIDELINES FOR ENLARGING OTHERS

The following six guidelines will help you in your efforts to enlarge others: be expressive, be sincere, be specific, be limited, be altruistic, and be persistent.

Be Expressive

The number one guideline is to be expressive, both nonverbally and verbally. No matter which enlarging technique you try, the important thing is to express it verbally to your loved one. All the kind, supportive, appreciative, loving, positive, or uplifting things you think for someone are of little good until you express them. Remember the motto "If you think it and it's good, express it!"

Be Sincere

No matter what you choose to share with your loved one, be sincere with your compliment, encouragement, or positive vision. Share only those comments that truly express what you think and how you feel. People generally can sense if you are being insincere and they will begin to distrust your statements in the future. Here are three questions you can ask yourself before you attempt to enlarge someone:

1. Do I believe this statement?
2. Do I want to share this statement with this individual?
3. Do I feel this statement will enlarge this individual?

If you answer no to any of these questions, think twice before sharing the comment. The purpose of enlarging statements is to make your loved one feel better. But if your loved one senses you're not being truthful or sincere, you've defeated your purpose. Share only those things you feel sincere about.

Be Specific

Make certain your comments are specific. The more specific the statement, the higher the probability the message will be received accurately by the other person. Vague, general statements leave too much room for misinterpretation and misunderstanding. A specific statement leaves much less to the imagination. Consider the following statements in both their general and specific forms, and decide which one communicates a clearer message and has a greater impact on you.

You're a really great person. (general)
I appreciate your smile and direct eye contact. (specific)

Thanks for everything. (general)
Thank you for your $25 contribution. (specific)

You look good. (general)
Your meditation has made you appear much more relaxed. (specific)

Be Limited

The fourth guideline for using enlarging statements is to limit them. By limit I mean don't go overboard with compliments and words of encouragement, especially if your loved ones aren't used to you saying anything positive or affirming.

Take it slow at first. You don't want to overload your loved ones with a stream of enlarging statements because you could easily overwhelm and confuse them. They might not know what to do with your radically altered way of communicating. Try one or two comments each day, until you get the feel of delivering enlarging statements. Once you feel comfortable delivering them and your loved ones become accustomed to receiving them, then you can gradually increase them. You don't want to scare the ones you love. You simply want to connect with them in positive ways that will make them feel better about themselves.

Be Altruistic

The fifth guideline is perhaps the most difficult. Be altruistic when you attempt to enlarge others. By altruistic, I mean you should enlarge others unselfishly, without expecting anything in return. That is truly a difficult task, to expect nothing in return. But you are more than capable of meeting the task. Instead, focus on giving a gift from your heart—the process of enlarging them. Be concerned about doing your best in your efforts to be enlarging, and detached from their responses to your good work. Your job is to see the best in your loved ones, communicate those things to them, and leave it at that—don't expect anything in return.

In my experience, happiness is something that happens to you when you're not looking for it. It's most often a by-product of an altruistic pursuit. It happens most often when you're concerned about the well-being of others and attempting to encourage and affirm them.

Be Persistent

You might want instant results and immediate appreciation for your attempts at enlarging others. We often wish people would notice that we are being more positive and encouraging. We hope they will tell us how much our compliments mean to them. We want them to grow, improve, and develop right before our eyes. But it usually doesn't happen that way. These things take time. Change is often slow in coming. So be persistent.

An old teacher of mine said, "You can either hurt or heal with your words." Your decision to give the gift of enlarging those you love can communicate acknowledgment, recognition, praise, encouragement, and optimism. You can choose to be the bearer of good news with your words and actions to those you love. And if you give the gift of enlarging others, you too will be changed by your efforts to enlarge others.

6.1 **Personal Exploration: Seeing the Best in Your Relationship**

Consider one relationship you are in and list five aspects of the relationship you feel are working (remember the 80/20 rule?).

Name of the individual: _____

Aspect 1: _____

Aspect 2: _____

Aspect 3: _____

Aspect 4: _____

Aspect 5: _____

6.2 **Practice Giving: Sharing the 80 Percent That Is Working**

During the next week, share the five aspects with the loved one you selected. Be as specific as possible.

What was his or her response? _____

_____

How did you feel sharing these items? _____

_____

6.3 **Practice Giving: Enlarging Others for One Day**

Select one day and consciously refuse to say anything negative about anyone or anything. Try to not even think negative thoughts. During these twenty-four hours, you can only enlarge other people by seeing and saying the best, acknowledging them, complimenting them, reframing negatives, and supporting them. Wow!

Were you able to be enlarging for twenty-four hours? _____

If not, what percentage of the time were you successful? _____

What was this experience like for you? _____

_____

Flowing with Conflict

〜

"The hard and strong will fall.
The soft and weak will overcome."
—Lao-tzu

As strawberry farmers in rural California, my mom and dad didn't have much time to explore the rolling foothills behind our house, wade through the muddy creek in search of frogs, or just sit against the trunk of an oak tree and watch the wind move silently through the summer grass. My mom and dad didn't always have the time, but I did.

Events of childhood are stored deep within the soul and their influence is felt in adulthood, often beneath the veil of consciousness. Memories, both joyous and sad, soothing and bitter, can tell us who we are.

One such memory for me occurred in my seventh year. My mom and dad were eating breakfast at the kitchen table in the quiet of the morning, long before sunrise. My four younger sisters were still asleep, but I was awake. From my bed I could see down the hallway into the kitchen where my parents were talking. Dad looked upset as he whispered to my mom across the little table.

Although I couldn't hear the conversation, I could tell they were having a disagreement. After talking for a while, my mom smiled, got up from her chair, and walked over to my father. She hugged him from behind as he laughed to himself.

This was not an isolated incident. That's how my parents handled their differences. The dance was usually the same. Whispering over morn-

ing coffee, a hug, and then laughter. I grew up thinking all parents re-solved conflict that way until I noticed my friends' parents often handled their differences in hurtful ways. Some yelled, some pouted, some cursed, and one man hit his wife. My eyes were opened as I observed other parents handle their conflict.

In junior high school I remember asking my mom if she and Dad ever fought with raised voices or fists.

"No," she told me. "I always have a choice when differences arise with your dad. I can become harder, or I can become softer. Marriage is a long haul," she continued, "and I decided during our first years together that I didn't want to harden, so I chose to soften and flow."

In any relationship, whether it's with your romantic partner, a family member, or a friend, inevitably conflict will arise. **Conflict** is any disagreement over two or more options. Conflict can be over where to go to lunch, how many children to raise, or the best way to get out of debt. Conflict is to be expected in any relationship. It's natural. The closer you get to another human being, the more conflict you experience. As you become more open and honest in any relationship, the differences between you and your loved one become more apparent. The areas of disagreement come to the surface and you are confronted with the fact that this other person does not think, believe, feel, and behave exactly the way you do. They are not you.

When differences arise, whether serious or not, some people react with raised voices while others choose to whisper. Some blame while others choose to explore. Some hit while others choose to listen. Some joke while others choose to brainstorm. How you decide to handle differences that eventually arise between you and someone you love speaks volumes about who you are and how you relate to others. What do you do when you disagree with a loved one?

The answer to this question is not a simple one. An individual's response to conflict is predicated on a variety of factors—the issue, the situation, the other individuals involved, what you want from the situation, and a myriad of other variables. To complicate matters further, many unconscious factors can also influence your response, such as your family of origin experiences, your deeper desires to control, direct, or distance your-self from the other, your emotional needs, and a host of other invisible forces.

RESPONSES TO CONFLICT

As a therapist, I have observed over the years that people take one of three characteristic stances or postures when conflict arises—fight, flight, or flow—although to varying degrees.

Fight

One characteristic response to conflict is to fight, where one person may blame, attack, criticize, argue, complain, find fault, or accuse. In extreme cases, he may physically harm the individual with whom he is in conflict. When he takes a fight response his body tenses, his breathing rate increases, and his movements can become exaggerated and swift. He is physically ready to defend himself or attack the enemy. He will often see the con-flict as a win-lose situation, where one person must win and the other must lose. The varieties of fight responses are many, but for our discussion the primary characteristic you need to remember is that the conflict is viewed as a fight with a winner and a loser. The individual who chooses to fight will battle with victory in mind.

Flight

The second response an individual might choose in a conflict is flight. The flight response can take many forms, but the goal is always the same—to avoid open conflict with another individual. The person may physically leave the room or the area of the conflict. She can also move to another town, state, or country to avoid constant conflict with a loved one.

Staying away from the home, whether it's working longer hours, going fishing, or volunteering at the Red Cross, can be another form of flight if the real purpose of such behavior is to avoid conflict.

Flight can also take a more subtle form, when an individual simply gives in to the demands, desires, or wishes of the other, against her own prefer-ence or better judgment. Being silent, agreeing, accommodating, placat-ing, pleasing, enabling, appeasing, or catering to the other person can be a form of conflict avoidance or taking flight.

Finally, flight can take physical form, such as psychosomatic illness, nervous breakdown, or suicide. These are all examples of ways people can avoid conflict by taking flight from the disagreement or situation.

Flow

The third response to conflict is to flow with it. In this response, the individual does not view conflict as bad or negative, but as natural. Conflict results from the fact that no two people are exactly the same. As individuals disclose more of who they are and what they want, their differences become more apparent.

Conflict is not a call to battle or a warning to end the relationship. Instead, conflict can be an invitation to listen, learn, explore, and grow with a loved one. Rather than fight or escape when disagreement arises, you might want to respond in a new way. Instead of tensing, relax. Instead of stiffening, bend. Instead of arguing, listen. Instead of pushing or running away, get closer. You can decide to flow with the disagreement, situation, or individual for a period to discover where it may lead.

Let's examine some specific ways you can flow with conflict rather than fight or avoid disagreements in your relationships.

WAYS TO FLOW WITH CONFLICT

Flowing with conflict is the gift of not fighting, resisting, blaming, or leaving. It is the gift of accepting and bending with the current of a disagreement for a period of time. Flowing with conflict can help a relationship to grow and even improve. Four ways to flow with conflict are to remain silent, restate the speaker's complaint, validate the speaker's feelings, and agree with the speaker's complaint.

Remain Silent

Usually when a conflict begins, we immediately respond by defending ourselves or redirecting the blame back to the other person. We interrupt the person and deny or redirect blame before he can finish his first sentence. We don't even give the speaker ten seconds to state his grievance or complaint. Many times our immediate interruptions serve only to escalate the disagreement, inflame the argument, or increase the speaker's commitment to his position.

You can respond very differently by remaining silent while your loved ones voice a complaint, regardless of your opinions or feelings about their remarks. By remaining silent, you can provide an opportunity for them to express their frustration or anger. You are detaching from your ego—your **self-centeredness** or concern for your own well-being—for this period of time and opening to their opinions and feelings. By choosing not to respond when an argument or disagreement begins, you are giving the gift of flowing with conflict.

Restate the Speaker's Complaint
The second way you can flow with conflict is to prove that you understand the person's complaint. Rather than immediately defending or attacking after you have remained silent for those initial moments and given the speaker a chance to talk, you can continue to flow with the conflict by restating the complaint.

Use your active listening skills when you find yourself in a conflict. By paraphrasing the complaint to the person's satisfaction, you have provided your loved one with the opportunity to be heard and understood. It might be enough to let the complaint be aired and comprehended. Here's an example of restating a complaint:

Tony: You always spend so much time at work. You never come home early and I'm stuck here with the kids all day long.

Betty: You'd like me to spend more time at home and less time at work?

The purpose of restating the complaint is not to solve the problem or declare your position. The goal is to simply restate the complaint so your loved one knows you understand what he is attempting to communicate.

Validate the Speaker's Feelings
A third way you can flow with conflict is to validate your loved one's feelings rather than discrediting or discounting them. Earlier we outlined the steps in active listening for feelings. In conflicts, the same process is extremely valuable. In addition to making certain that you understand the complaint, it's important to validate your loved one's feelings about the complaint.

By validating feelings, we go one step further than merely reflecting a loved one's feelings. We confirm and support her feelings as being valid and legitimate. Remember, this process of flowing with conflict requires a spirit of giving and an attitude of **other-centeredness**—concern for the well-being of another person. It's not about you and your feelings at this point of the conflict. Your concern is for your loved one and you can show this by validating his feelings. Here's an example of validating the speaker's feelings:

David: You don't ever seem to ask me how I feel about how we should get out of debt.

Chris: Are you feeling angry that we don't talk about our finances?

The purpose of validating the speaker's feelings is to let the speaker know that you understand the feelings and acknowledge the feelings as legitimate. There's no effort invested in negating or disconfirming the feelings. Your goal is to validate them.

Agree with the Speaker's Complaint

You can really surprise your loved one by agreeing with the complaint being shared with you. There is usually some truth to any complaint or accusation a loved one brings to our attention, no matter how vehemently we would like to deny or dismiss the charge. You don't need to agree with the entire complaint, just the portion you can accept. Usually, we deny the entire complaint or accuse the speaker of the same. But if you can really listen to what the speaker is saying and try to find some truth that you can agree with, the direction of the conflict can take an entirely new course. Here are a few examples of agreeing with the speaker's complaint:

Robin: You're always late to every meeting.

Shae: You're right. I am late to many of the meetings.

Cindy: That was a foolish thing to do. I would never do that!

Sam: That was a pretty foolish thing to do.

Edna: You don't listen to me when I'm upset.

Vera: I really haven't listened to you like I want to.

By agreeing with whatever truth there might be to the complaint, you can bring about a new and different pattern to your usual way of fighting or arguing. This alone may be effective in changing the speaker's feelings.

By remaining silent, restating the speaker's complaint, validating the speaker's feelings, and agreeing with the speaker's complaint during the initial stages of conflict, you can create a supportive environment for discussing and resolving a conflict rather than resisting, attacking, or leaving. After you have established this supportive climate, you can try a technique I've developed called the SLACK Method to resolve conflict.

THE SLACK METHOD
FOR RESOLVING CONFLICT

The SLACK Method provides a win/win approach to resolving conflicts— one that involves negotiation and compromise. This technique works for serious conflicts, as well as for minor disagreements. The five steps to the SLACK Method are:

Sit

Listen

Ask

Compromise

Kiss

I've been teaching this technique in therapy and in relationship courses for more than fifteen years, and it has been successful in helping people negotiate satisfying solutions to problems in a way that strengthens their relationships. Let's take a look at each of these steps.

Step 1: Sit
The first thing you do when a conflict occurs is to sit down. Somehow a standing position gets us into a combative stance and can often escalate the conflict. Try breaking this habit of standing. A seated posture will relax and center you both. So sit down. Take a load off your feet. You'll be doing some serious work in a few minutes.

If possible, retreat to a quiet place where you won't be disturbed. My wife and I go to the master bathroom. It has a lock on the door and the kids can't get in.

Agree on a time limit for the session. Usually ten to twenty minutes is a reasonable amount of time for one session. You don't want to go more than twenty minutes, because the effort involved requires a great deal of concentration and can be emotionally draining. Don't think you have to settle this once and for all in one sitting. Things take time. Be gentle on yourselves. Don't go more than twenty minutes.

Before you begin Step 2, take a minute or two to sit silently and calm yourselves. Breathe deeply and evenly. Close your eyes. You may want to visualize a peaceful scene. I usually visualize Sea Cliff Beach, near our home. Do whatever centers you. It will get you in the right frame of mind. Remember, conflict is an invitation to know your partner in a deeper way and strengthen the relationship. Keep your heart soft and your ears open as you enter Step 2.

Step 2: LISTEN

The second step requires you to listen to your partner for one to three minutes without verbal interruption. Your partner can hold a pencil as a reminder that she has the "microphone." During this time, your partner:

1. Describes her perceptions of the issue. (I see the issue as _____.)
2. Shares her feelings about the issue. (I feel _____.)
3. States her need(s) regarding the issue. (I need _____.)
4. Reveals her fear(s) about the issue. (And I'm afraid that _____.)

You are not to interrupt in any way. You cannot talk. You cannot blame, judge, criticize, bring up past mistakes, or discuss another issue. All you do is sit silently and listen to her. By remaining silent, you will avoid the single, worst mistake in conflict communication—interrupting the speaker. As you're listening, remember to avoid any negative or critical behaviors, such as shaking your head, rolling your eyes, or scowling. These negative non-verbal behaviors can discourage communication as much as any verbal criticism or negative remark.

When your partner feels she has finished, she will say, "Okay, let's go to Step 3." Remember, you can't talk until she gives you the okay.

Step 3: ASK

In the third step you paraphrase or reflect your partner's statements from Step 2. (Remember this from Gift 4?) Ask the following questions to prove you understand her perceptions and feelings:

1. You see the issue as _____? (Let her respond.)
2. You are feeling _____? (Let her respond.)
3. You need _____? (Let her respond.)
4. You're afraid that _____? (Let her respond.)

The purpose of Step 3 is not to give your side of the story but to prove you are attempting to understand your loved one. You are trying to demonstrate that you've heard her perceptions and feelings of the issue. Many times, this alone is enough to change the dynamics of the situation. It's impossible to overemphasize how important it is for people to feel as if they've been truly heard and understood. This by itself is significant and casts a healing glow over the entire process.

When your partner feels that you understand her perceptions, feelings, needs, and fears, she will give you the "microphone" and you can return to Step 2 for your turn. You now have a chance to share your perceptions, feelings, needs, and fears of the problem without your partner interrupting. Remember, you now have the "microphone."

After you have finished, you will say, "Okay, let's go to Step 3" and your partner will ask *you* questions about *your* statements. When you feel your partner has accurately reflected all four of your statements, go to Step 4.

Step 4: COMPROMISE

Now that you and your partner have completed Steps 2 and 3, you are in a position to better understand each other's feelings and concerns about the conflict. The next step is to find a compromise.

Before you compromise, you must each brainstorm two or three solutions you would be willing to try and then share them with each other. Brainstorming several solutions ensures that neither of you is too attached to one solution, making a compromise easier. When you share the solutions, do not evaluate or criticize. Simply listen to each other just as you did in Step 2. You'll have at least four solutions to consider. Discuss the solutions to explore their strengths and weaknesses. Ask for clarification.

You might both decide on one that is worth trying. If not, select your favorite solution from your partner's list. This lets your partner know you think at least one of her solutions is worthwhile. Your partner should select the solution she likes best from your list also.

Try to compromise on a solution that lies somewhere between the two favorite solutions. Maybe you would both be willing to try one of the solutions for a period of time. Keep in mind that this is a tentative compromise that can be modified or dropped if it does not work. Chances are that neither you nor your partner will get your number-one choice. But you most likely will find a solution you can both "live with for a time." Remember, a win/win, not a win/lose compromise is the goal of the SLACK Method for resolving conflict. Also set up an implementation schedule and a time period to try the solution. When you have agreed on a solution and implementation plan, go to the final step.

If you cannot reach a compromise in Step 4 and you're running out of time or steam, take a break for an hour or a day, but go to Step 5 anyway. Be gentle on yourselves. Many conflicts have taken months and years to develop. Give yourselves plenty of time to resolve or improve the situation. Go to the final step no matter how far you are from a compromise.

Step 5: Kiss

End the session with a compliment or two to your partner (and a kiss or hug if you feel it's appropriate). Spend a few minutes discussing the strengths of the relationship and things you would miss if it ended. Remember the 80/20 rule? Look for and focus on the 80 percent of the relationship you can commend or compliment.

That's the SLACK Method for solving conflict. Give it a try the next time you find yourself in a conflict with a loved one. This technique provides a simple, constructive, and effective means for resolving conflict.

GUIDELINES FOR RESOLVING CONFLICT

Whenever you attempt to resolve a conflict with a loved one, remember the following seven guidelines: keep the relationship in mind; limit the conflict to one issue; think of conflict as an invitation to growth; state fears, not ultimatums; be flexible; separate the behavior from the person; and be soft and slow.

Keep the Relationship in Mind

While you are in a conflict, keep the relationship foremost in your mind. Very few conflicts are worth ending a relationship for, and you need to remind yourself of this fact as you try to solve your differences.

One way I keep this in mind is to ask myself, "Would I rather be right or be in a loving relationship that could last forever?" This question keeps whatever issue my wife and I are discussing in the proper perspective. In fact, this question is helpful in keeping any conflict in its proper perspective. Be flexible and spacious. A good relationship is worth all the effort in the world, and very few differences are important enough to end a loving relationship.

Limit the Conflict to One Issue

One of the most common mistakes in attempting to solve a conflict is to bring into the discussion other areas of disagreement in the relationship. In the heat of an argument, it's tempting to bring up other problems. If you and your loved one are discussing where to spend Thanksgiving, his folks or yours, don't slip in the fact that you don't like the dent in the car door he made accidentally with his golf club and his weakness for chocolates. Stick to just one issue at a time. Focusing on a single issue will help you both find an acceptable solution to your problem more quickly. Don't get sidetracked with other issues.

And while we're at it, don't bring up past mistakes either. We all have our favorite gripe or grudge about a loved one, and often it's tempting to bring up that issue when tempers are flying. Don't. Old baggage weighs down the conversation with unnecessary and counterproductive material.

Think of Conflict as an Invitation to Grow

Conflict is not something to be avoided at all costs. Conflict is an invitation to grow—to learn to listen to another person, to empathize, to negotiate, to compromise, to give up ground, and to become gentler with others and ourselves.

Just keep in mind all conflict is a chance for you and loved ones to examine your relationship more closely, to pay attention to one another's needs and wants, and to become better friends than you are now. Because we are forever changing, relationships need to keep growing. And conflict provides an opportunity to enhance any relationship.

State Fears, Not Ultimatums

When you and your loved ones are communicating about a conflict, be careful not to state ultimatums too quickly or too often. I believe we have a tendency to issue ultimatums too quickly when we're in conflicts. "Do it my way or else," "Shape up or ship out," and "If you don't let me talk, you'll be sleeping on the couch" are some examples of ultimatums.

But in most circumstances do ultimatums really improve our relationships? No. In fact, ultimatums accomplish just the opposite. They serve to cement your loved one's position even more firmly. They instill defensiveness and resentment in the relationship. And most times they are an unnecessary display of power. Reserve ultimatums for only the most serious circumstances.

Rather than attempting to resolve a conflict with an ultimatum, try stating a fear you have about the conflict. For example, instead of telling your partner, "Either you drop your college class or I'll leave your suitcase on the doorstep" (ultimatum), you might say, "I'm afraid if you get your college degree, you'll be bored with me and leave me" (stating fear). Notice the big difference between the ultimatum the speaker issued in the first example and the fear he shared in the second example?

The advantage of stating your fears instead of issuing ultimatums is that fear statements are easier to give up. You don't want to hold on to fear statements. If your partner responded, "Of course I'd never leave you. The reason I'm going to college is to become a better person for myself and for you," you would be more likely to give up the fear of your partner leaving than to enforce the ultimatum. Your loved one is more likely to come to your aid and dispel an unfounded fear you are feeling, rather than line up for battle against your ultimatum.

Be Flexible

When you and your loved one are compromising, be as yielding as possible. We often view compromise as weakness and yielding as giving up or giving in. But nothing could be further from the truth. The finest, most satisfying, and healthiest relationships are characterized by flexibility.

Separate the Behavior from the Person

In a conflict, we often tend to lump the behavior that is annoying us with the person doing the behavior. Instead of saying, "I get upset when you come home late" or "I feel rejected when you don't call me," we often criticize or condemn the person by saying, "You're a jerk!" or "I hate you!"

A better reaction is to separate the person from the behavior you dislike. I've found it useful to distinguish between these categories by saying, "I love you (person), but I don't like it when you come home late (behavior)" or "I really like you (person) and I feel rejected when you don't call me when you promised would (behavior)."

This simple technique of communicating your feelings about the person and then stating your feelings about an action is very helpful in separating the person from the behavior.

Be Soft and Slow

One of the most difficult things to do when we're in the midst of conflict is to talk in a slow and soft tone of voice. This is one of the last things we want to do. Everything tells us to speed up, to tighten up, to gear up. Often our breathing becomes fast and shallow, our face becomes flushed, and our speech becomes rapid and loud.

These nonverbal behaviors trigger similar responses in our loved one. Before long the discussion turns into a heated screaming match, diminishing the prospect for a mutually satisfying solution to the conflict. You need to remind yourself to speak in a slow, gentle tone of voice. This will help keep the discussion on track and the atmosphere more supportive and relaxed. You will find it helpful to breathe deeply as you speak and listen. Don't hold your breath. Don't tighten your shoulders and neck. Just breathe deeply and evenly, no matter what is being said.

According to an old Japanese saying, "The one who raises his voice first loses the argument." Soft and slow—that's the secret.

Conflict is a natural part of any long-term relationship. Try flowing with conflict the next time you and loved ones have differences of opinion or struggle over options. By flowing with conflict, rather than defending, fighting, or fleeing, you will be opening up an entirely new set of options and possibilities. Conflict can take you and your loved ones down a different, more positive path on your relationship journey.

$\backsim$

7.1 Personal Exploration: Reflecting on a Recent Conflict

Recall a conflict you had with a loved one. Try to remember what it was about, your feelings, your response, and the outcome.

1. What was the conflict? _____

2. What were your feelings at the time? _____

3. What was your response?　　fight　　flight　　flow

4. What was the outcome? _____

5. How could you have flowed with this conflict?

_____

_____

7.2 Practice Giving: Receiving Feedback on Your Conflict Style

Ask a loved one who knows you well for feedback on how you typically handle conflict. Your goal is to receive information about your conflict style. Ask the following questions:

1. What is my usual conflict response style—fight, flight, or flow?
2. How do you feel about my conflict response style?
3. How might I improve my conflict resolution efforts?

Describe the feedback you received and your response to it.

_____

_____

7.3 Practice Giving: Resolving Conflict

The next time you and a loved one have a minor conflict, try using the SLACK Method to resolve it. Keep in mind the seven guidelines for resolving conflict as you work through the SLACK Method.

Describe your response to the SLACK Method.

_____

_____

Showing You Care

∽

"If love is real, it will be evident in our daily lives,
in the many ways we show we care."
–Thich Nhat Hanh

My friend's husband died of leukemia fifteen years ago. Russ's death left Sharon with a broken heart and a four-year-old daughter to raise on her own. Russ was an outgoing man whose expressive nature let Sharon know just how loved she was. I especially admired the way he showed his love for his wife and daughter by his actions more than his words. I always noticed his ever-present smile, kind eyes, and gentle touch that declared his love for Sharon and Emma.

Five years after Russ's death, my wife and I were having lunch with Sharon in a quiet Chinese restaurant. I asked Sharon what she missed most about Russ.

"I miss his warm toes on my cold feet when I'd wake up at night."

"His toes?" I smiled in disbelief.

"Oh, yeah," Sharon said. "His warm feet against my cold toes. There are a lot of things I miss about Russ, but just being able to feel his warm feet is what I miss most in the middle of the night."

My wife added, "I know the feeling. I'd miss Randy's hugs at night the most, right before we fall asleep."

Since that conversation, I've thought a lot about what I'd miss most about Vicky. It would be the way she smiles at me right before she falls asleep at night. I've seen that smile countless nights over the years—a soft, timeless smile from the one who knows me better than anyone else in this world.

You know, I guess I know the feeling too!

⌒

Perhaps the most memorable gifts we give are not communicated by words, but by our bodies. Although our verbal expressions of love and caring are essential, it is our body language that truly connects us with the hearts of those we love. It's that knowing smile, the gentle kiss, the familiar hug, and even the warmth of well-known toes in the middle of the night, that show you care. The language of the body is deep and quiet, speaking to the parts of our soul that transcend language and thought itself.

No matter with whom you are connecting—romantic partner, family member, or friend—body language provides the most intimate, powerful form of communication. Whether it's the reassuring pat on the back from a friend, the gentle kiss of a mother, or the familiar touch of a lover, body language conveys an important message—the gift of showing you care.

Recall that nonverbal communication is neither spoken nor written. It is communicated by posture, clothing, voice, touch, gestures, face, and eyes. It is your physical presence, the distance you stand from others, your punctuality or tardiness. It's the appearance of your desk, the interior of your car, and the jewelry you wear. Studies in nonverbal communication would suggest that it's not what we say that's important, but what we do.

WAYS TO SHOW YOU CARE

Once you get the hang of it, you can spend your entire lifetime discovering new and creative ways to show you care. There are hundreds of ways to show you care, but let's start with these nine: be present, do nothing, touch, hug, smile, speak gently, keep promises, stay in touch, and laugh at yourself.

Be Present
The most important aspect of being present is that you are physically with those you love. You don't have to necessarily do anything special. Your partner might enjoy just sitting in silence at the beach or strolling around the

neighborhood after dinner. And your mom or dad might be delighted if you dropped by and treated them to a late-afternoon milk shake. It doesn't really matter what you do with your loved ones as long as you spend unstructured, enjoyable time together.

Take stock of how you spend an average week. Chart each day, hour by hour, with your activities—sleeping, working, commuting, eating, shopping, playing, spending time with loved ones, and so forth. You'd be surprised how little time you actually devote to being with those you love. You might need to rearrange your priorities to devote more time with your loved ones. What are some ways you can spend extra time with your loved ones?

Regular dates. One popular way to spend more time together is to arrange regular dates. Actually set aside one evening each week to spend time with your spouse or partner and another evening or afternoon with your children, parents, friends, or other loved ones.

At our house, Vicky and I reserve Thursday evenings to go on a date. We have a baby-sitter who stays with our two boys from 6 P.M. to 10 P.M. Friday nights are designated our "$20 family night"—one of the four of us plans an evening of fun and entertainment that cannot exceed twenty dollars. And most Saturday mornings, my two sons and I go out for breakfast to talk about their week and then go surfing if the waves are good.

Check-in time. Another simple way to be present for your loved one is to set aside a special ten-minute "check-in" time before you go to work and again before you go to bed. You and a loved one can sit together where you won't be interrupted and share how you're both doing. This may mean getting up ten or fifteen minutes earlier and going to bed a few minutes later each day, but the results will be well worth the effort. You may not be able to go out on a date every evening, but these little "check-in" times are equally valuable in reestablishing those connections that show you care.

No matter what you decide to do with the time you devote to your loved ones, just make certain that you give the gift of showing you care by being present. You'll never regret the time you spent with them.

Do Nothing

One very important nonverbal message you can communicate to your loved one is to do nothing. I know this may sound strange, but doing nothing can be a very loving and powerful message. Communicate trust in what your loved one is doing by not intervening, redirecting, evaluating, instructing, or correcting.

A woman in one of my classes shared the story about her first attempt to wax a car. She had been married for less than a year and she wanted to surprise her husband by washing and waxing his car while he was napping one afternoon. While she was applying the wax onto the car, her husband woke and walked out to the driveway where she was rubbing wax onto the hood of the car. He grabbed the rag from her hand, complaining how she wasn't using the proper circular motion. Without saying a word, she walked back into the house. He followed her up the front steps, asking her why she was upset, but she didn't respond. She just kept walking.

It would have been better for the husband to do nothing—to simply sit on the front porch and watch his wife apply the wax (even the wrong way) and appreciate the real message of her actions. Instead he put down her efforts.

We might have been taught to do things the "right" way. And to make matters worse, we might still feel compelled to teach others the "correct" or "right" way to do something. Whether it's making bread, inputting data into a computer, or waxing a car, we feel it's our responsibility to instruct others on the proper method.

There are times when intervention is necessary, especially in cases of physical or emotional abuse. Yet one of the most loving behaviors you can demonstrate is to do nothing, to silently accept what your loved one is doing, even when you disagree with his or her behavior. We need to develop our ability to do nothing. Not only in minor matters, like waxing cars, but in more important matters—when a loved one wants to take a class at the community college, learn to fly an airplane, or explain why he or she is upset with us. During these times we need to nonverbally give our loved ones space to decide what's best for them. We need to trust their actions, to acknowledge their decisions, and to let them apply the wax, even if it's the "wrong" way. A loving relationship is always more important than a perfectly shined car.

Touch
Touching provides the most immediate and powerful form of connection we can establish with another human being. No other form of communi-

cation is as intimate. The comfort of a friend's arm over your shoulder, the intimacy of sexual union, and the feel of someone's warm toes in the night are just a few ways we can connect with another person through the experience of touch—skin to skin contact.

Many people complain that they'd like to touch more but don't know exactly what to do. Well, for those folks, here's a list of some touching behaviors you might want to try. In addition to holding hands and touching a shoulder, you can pat, stroke, tickle, rub, massage, and

wrap your arm around a waist
place your hand on a back
walk arm in arm
wipe a brow
groom hair
straighten a collar
warm a foot
rub a cheek
massage a neck
slap a back
tickle a chin
clasp a hand

and a hundred other things to connect with your loved one. Don't get caught up in doing it the "right" way. Just try to increase your touching behavior. Go slowly. Don't rush things. Many of us, because of culture or family habits, are not inclined to be touchers. So our attempts to initiate or increase our touching behavior must be done gradually. Try to initiate two touching behaviors during the next seven days. You can hold hands with your best friend for two or three minutes while you're walking together. You can simply touch your friends' shoulders when you speak with them during the same seven days. That's the way you're going to connect with those you love.

You can give the gift of touching to those you love and build those bridges of connection that words can never achieve. Take a moment right now and look at your palms and fingers. These two hands can initiate deeper relationships with loved ones if you only reach out and make those intimate connections.

Hug

Hugging is another way we can show caring to those we love. When I was younger, I restricted my hugging to my wife, my mother, and my four sisters. Over the years, however, I've come to enjoy hugging my dad, my brothers-in-law, my male and female friends, my colleagues, and just about anyone else I feel connected to. There was a time I thought hugging should be reserved for only a select few. But now I'm beginning to realize its literal and symbolic power to connect me to those I care for.

No other form of physical contact, short of sexual union, places us in such immediate and intimate contact with another human being. When we hug, we feel the other person, we smell the other person, and we hear their words in our ears. We need to greet and say farewell with a hug. Hug those you love!

Smile

This should be obvious, but you never know...

Your decision to smile at others is one of the most significant decisions you make moment to moment, day in and day out, year after year. If you smile at others, they will more than likely return your smile. If you don't smile, they will be less likely to smile at you. This sounds pretty simple, yet we need to be reminded of this. A smile shows you care. Most of us think we offer a cheerful countenance to our loved ones, but you'd be surprised how often we're mistaken.

Increasing our smiling is something we should all do. How can we smile more? One technique I have my students try is to use a mirror to provide immediate feedback when speaking on the telephone. They place a small mirror on their desk so they can see their faces as they talk. This gives them an immediate picture of their smiling behavior.

I know this may sound silly, but when I've conducted communication seminars for real-estate agents, this little mirror trick is the most popular (and effective) suggestion I offer to increase their rapport with perspective clients. I'm not suggesting you wear a mirror around your neck when talking to people, but the next time you're talking to your loved one, place a mirror in front of you and see how much smiling you actually do. You might be surprised.

Another technique you might want to try to smile more frequently is to have your loved ones provide feedback on your behavior. Let's say you ask your sister to silently point to her lip when you're frowning or displaying a blank look. This is your signal to smile. You'd be surprised how this feedback can increase your smiling. And just as important, it lets your loved one know you're trying to improve your supportive communication with her, which is possibly more important than the behavior itself.

Smile. It shows you care.

Speak Gently

Have you ever thought of your voice as the thermometer of your emotional temperature? When you're angry, your voice communicates hostility and aggression. And when you're excited, your voice communicates elation and anticipation. No matter what words you choose to speak, your voice communicates emotional messages. It's the real message beneath the verbal message. Your voice says more about how you're feeling than do your words.

What does your voice say about you? Is your voice gentle, soothing, and relaxed? Or is it rushed, irritating, and wearied? There are times we need to speak in soft, calm, and caring tones. Delivering the language of love needs to be different than directing firefighters to the second floor of a burning building or leading an assault on the front lines of a battlefield.

One woman complained that her husband would always yell at her. He was the lead foreman of a large construction crew and he would scream commands, directions, and criticism to his workers ten to twelve hours a day. When he got home from work, he spoke to his wife and children in the same harsh, loud way.

During a therapy session with the couple, I videotaped one of their discussions and then played the tape to them. The husband was startled at the loud, harsh tone of voice he used when speaking to his wife. He had never heard his own voice on tape before. At his insistence, the next two sessions were spent softening his way of speaking and the manner in which he interacted with family members.

If we are to truly communicate caring with our actions, we need to be sensitive to the manner in which we talk to our loved ones. Our **paralanguage**—the way we talk—should be softer and slower. These two characteristics of talking are important if we are to communicate caring.

How can we discover what our voice sounds like to those we love? Just get a tape recorder and record five minutes of a conversation with a friend.

Talk about a variety of subjects during the five-minute period—the highlight of your day, something that upset you, and what you had for lunch. After you've talked, play back the recording and listen carefully to your voice. Does it sound like you? Do you sound warm or cold? Are your words fast or slow? Are you speaking too fast or is the speed just right? Do you sound sincere? Do you like your voice? Ask your friend what he or she thinks of your voice.

Practice speaking more slowly and more softly into the recorder. Play your conversation back and see how your voice sounds with these modifications. Experiment with your voice, using the recorder as your tool for change. Remember, many times it's not what you say, but how you say it. Show you care by speaking gently.

Keep Promises

Many years ago I was lying on the Kaui beach in front of our hotel while my wife, Vicky, was taking a nap in our room. I struck up a conversation with an old Hawaiian fisherman named Herbie. He was a retired sugar plantation foreman and, for a man of 82, he looked slim, trim, and happy. After learning I was vacationing with my wife, Herbie told me he was going on his forty-seventh year of a wonderful marriage! He told me the secret to his long marriage was keeping promises. "Always keep your promises to your wife," he said. "The big things and the small things—it doesn't matter. Keep your promises. Trust is the name of the game."

As we talked, Herbie gave me a specific bit of advice. He said, "If you're going to be late coming home from work, even just ten minutes, give your wife a call. It shows you respect her."

Over the years, I've put Herbie's advice to use. Even the one about calling my wife if I'm going to be late. And you know, it works for us. Vicky even brags about my "being late" phone calls to her friends.

At a deeper level, your decision to keep promises to loved ones is the basis for your overall credibility. When you promise to take your aunt out to dinner on Tuesday night, do you come through? When you promise to do a favor for a friend, do you follow through? When you promise your grandfather you'll call, do you keep your word?

Here are a couple of hints I've collected from students and clients who were pretty good at keeping promises. First, don't promise something you don't intend or aren't able to keep. Sometimes we promise more than we know we can deliver on. It's better to keep your mouth shut and not break a promise than to promise the moon and not be able or willing to deliver.

Second, don't make too many promises in a given day. Keep your promises to a minimum so you can focus your energy on keeping them. Once again, it's better to make one or two promises and deliver on them than to make a bunch of promises and deliver on none of them.

Third, keep track of your promises either in your head (which is difficult at best) or on paper. One man in my class told us he keeps any promise he makes to his wife or children on a little 39¢ notepad and scratches off each promise when he completes it. This may be going a bit too far, but I bet his wife and kids appreciate his efforts to show he cares.

And finally, when you can't keep a promise, let your loved one know it as soon as possible. Don't try to hide the fact or pretend you don't remember making the promise in the first place. That just makes matters worse. Be mature enough to admit it and apologize. We can't always make good on everything we promise, but we need to show we care by admitting it when we don't.

Stay in Touch

I once worked with a middle-aged woman in therapy who was in the process of grieving her husband's recent death. She said something I've never forgotten: "One of the things I miss most about Ed is his lunchtime telephone calls. For more than thirteen years, he would call me for a minute or two during his lunch break and tell me he loved me. Every lunch hour for thirteen years! I miss the little ways he kept in touch."

Staying in touch is another nonverbal way we can communicate caring to our loved ones. We don't have to be on a business trip halfway around the world to think about keeping in touch. It's these daily reminders we appreciate and remember. Whether it's a phone call during a lunch break, a little note on the steering wheel of your partner's car, or a love letter sent from your workplace, these are ways we show caring. Be on the lookout for new ways to stay in touch during your day with those you love.

In fact, why don't you just give yourself a break and put the book down. Go over to your phone, yes, right this moment, and give your loved one a call for no particular reason. Just call to say hello and connect for a moment or two. This phone call might be the most significant act you will do this entire day. Go ahead, make that call!

Laugh at Yourself

The final way to show you care is to laugh at yourself. Can you laugh at your own shortcomings? Do you possess the ability to poke fun at yourself? Are you willing to lighten up occasionally and smile at an unusual mannerism or habit you have?

From a psychological point of view, your ability to laugh at yourself displays a healthy willingness to detach from your ego, your self-image. You probably expend enormous energy and effort to protect yourself from unfair criticism, attack, and aggression. You take yourself seriously, and you should. There's work to do, money to earn, and goals to accomplish. This is all fine and well, but are you willing to let go occasionally and smile at your funny mannerisms, weird habits, and unusual quirks? We need to balance seriousness and lightheartedness. Can you detach from your serious, protective self, and periodically smile good-naturedly at yourself?

This ability is especially valuable during interpersonal conflict. When you and a loved one are attempting to resolve a dispute and he says, "You're really being grouchy!" your natural inclination is to defend yourself or return the attack. But if you feel there's some truth to what is said, can you let go long enough to breathe, smile good-naturedly, and say, "You're right. I'm being an old grouch. Sorry." Can you detach from your serious self? Can you occasionally let go of winning every argument?

You may object to this notion and view any willingness to laugh at yourself as a weakness or fault. I believe that in your attempts to communicate for connection with loved ones, this willingness to not take yourself seriously all the time is one of the healthiest gifts you can give.

We need to admit we're not perfect. We need to give ourselves permission to make mistakes, have faults, and be downright weird sometimes. Who's keeping score anyway? We need to learn to take ourselves less seriously and not be number one in all things. Maybe if we develop the willingness and ability to laugh at ourselves more often, the journey to the hearts of our loved ones will be easier to navigate. Lighten up.

GUIDELINES FOR SHOWING YOU CARE

Before you toss this book aside and begin hugging everyone you know, you might want to take a deep breath and relax. Here are a few guidelines to consider when giving the gift of showing you care:

Be Sensitive to Social and Cultural Differences

Much of our nonverbal communication is universal and its meaning is interpreted similarly from culture to culture. For instance, smiling, laughter, and crying behavior are understood universally. A smile in Japan communicates the same message as a smile in the United States. And crying in Brazil communicates the same message as crying in the Netherlands.

One common mistake we make, however, is to believe that all of our nonverbal communication behavior is expressed and interpreted similarly in all social settings and cultures. This is not the case for all behaviors. Direct eye contact in the United States is most often interpreted as a positive, confident, and open way of communicating with another person, whereas Asians and Northern Europeans view direct eye contact as rude and invasive. You can see where even a simple behavior such as eye contact between individuals from two different cultures could result in some very disturbing miscommunication.

When communicating with loved ones, be sensitive to any social or cultural norms of nonverbal communication that might be relevant. The specific nonverbal behaviors presented in this chapter are based on the norms in the United States. But even in the United States, you need to be aware of and sensitive to social and cultural differences when you communicate with others.

When in Doubt, Do a Perception Check

Given the enormous amount of nonverbal communication available in one message and the complexity of any single communication event, it is no wonder that nonverbal communication is often difficult to decipher.

Let's imagine that your coworker begins to increase eye contact with you during a one-week period. How do you interpret this change in behavior? Does this behavior mean romantic attraction, new contact lenses, or disapproval of your new haircut? Who knows what to make of it? A single nonverbal behavior such as increased eye contact may have many different meanings. Nonverbal communication can be very ambiguous.

One important way to find out what a particular behavior means is to simply ask the individual. By **perception checking**—comparing your perceptions with those of another—you can shed some light on your confusion. You can say, "I've noticed this past week that you've been looking in my direction more than usual. Is my haircut that ugly?" This lets the coworker know your concern and your interpretation, and provides him with the opportunity to give you his response. It might be, "Heck no! I've been watching the construction on the building outside your window" or "Yes, your hair is so wild, I can't help but stare." Your invitation to check perceptions lets you clarify ambiguous nonverbal behavior.

Take It Slowly

A final reminder before you begin showing you care is to take it slowly. By that I mean don't overwhelm your loved ones with a dramatic or startling change in your nonverbal behavior. For instance, if you've never hugged your father before and begin by hugging and kissing him with reckless abandon, he may react to your behavior with defensiveness or even hostility. Take it slow. Begin small. Try one hug for openers. Then maybe try two the next meeting. Build up gradually if it feels appropriate and comfortable for both parties. This advice goes for all the ways to show caring presented here. Take it slowly.

Talk is cheap. Your behavior really communicates your caring. One of the most important gifts from your heart is showing you care in ways your loved ones can see, feel, and touch. Whether it's turning down a job promotion so you can spend more time with your family or just giving someone a hug, your nonverbal communication can express your caring to others. In the end, you won't regret spending less time at the office and more time with your loved ones. Decide to give the gift of showing you care.

‿

8.1 **Personal Exploration: Who Showed You Love?**

It is always helpful to reflect on those people in our lives who have shown they loved us and cared for us. Take a moment to list three specific individuals who showed they cared for you by doing something specific. They can be a parent, relative, teacher, coach, friend, or neighbor. Often, when we can identify individuals who have shown us love, we are more likely to turn around and do the same for our loved ones.

1. _____ loved me by _____

2. _____ loved me by _____

3. _____ loved me by _____

How do you feel about the impact these three individuals have made on your life?

_____

_____

_____

_____

8.2 Practice Giving: Increasing Your Touch

Increase your touching behavior with a loved one for one week. Try to use at least three of the nine touching behaviors we discussed during the next seven days.

What did it feel like to increase your touching behavior?

_____

_____

_____

_____

How did your loved one respond to your increased touching?

_____

_____

_____

_____

8.3 Practice Giving: Laughing at Yourself (a little)

List three things about yourself that you think are humorous, funny, embarrassing, or downright ridiculous. If you can't list three, there's something wrong with you. Either you're perfect, in denial, or just plain uptight. Loosen up just a little and fill in the blanks below. It will be good for you.

1. _____

2. _____

3. _____

Encouraging Growth

〜

"It is difficult to grow and develop
without the encouragement of others."
–Arthur Gordon

The Monday following Thanksgiving is a favorite day for my wife and me. That's the day we pile our two boys, the dog, and a picnic lunch into our pickup and head to the Christmas tree farm. As we wind through the backroads of the Santa Cruz mountains, the leaves splash bright yellow and orange against the crisp autumn sky. The sign marking the entrance to the Christmas tree farm is barely noticeable from the road, yet it's cheerful and festive, just like the woman who runs the place.

Marjorie had been a legal secretary for eighteen years and her husband was an engineer for IBM. After their children were grown, Marjorie began talking about doing something different—very different. Marjorie wanted to work on a Christmas tree farm!

Most husbands would have laughed at the idea. Some would have gotten irritated or at least refused to give it serious consideration. But not Ron. Ron not only listened to her dream, he encouraged Marjorie to explore her desire to work with Christmas trees.

After three years of working part-time on a Christmas tree farm, Marjorie shared with Ron her dream of owning a Christmas tree farm. After much discussion and research, they agreed to give it a try. They looked for an established tree farm in the Santa Cruz mountains with a house on the property for them to live in. Marjorie would run the farm and Ron would commute to his job. Within a year and a half, Marjorie and Ron had sold their home in town and were the proud owners of an eight-acre Christmas tree farm! That was seven years ago.

I once asked Majorie if her husband enjoyed working on the Christmas tree farm with her.

"No. Ron doesn't like this kind of work. He pitches in when I need the help. But most of the time, I run the farm with my hired man."

"Does Ron have any regrets?" I asked.

"No," she chuckled. "Ron's a rare man. He's always encouraged me, believed in me. He loves me in the way that counts the most—he wants the best for me."

〜

Ron is a rare man indeed. We don't often listen to or encourage the dreams of our loved ones. We often discourage, ridicule, and even prohibit our loved ones' explorations to dream or grow in a new direction. Whether their dream involves going back to school, learning to skydive, taking up a new hobby, wanting to be the president of the United States, or wanting to own a Christmas tree farm, we are often unwilling to encourage them. Usually we tend to support only those ventures we can share.

One secret for building loving relationships is encouraging growth—to inspire our loved ones to explore their dreams. Not only can we accept and acknowledge their desires to change and grow, we can also help them experiment with activities that may make their dreams a reality. This is a profound gift from the heart—encouraging growth in a loved one.

PRINCIPLES FOR GROWING IN RELATIONSHIPS

One common myth about relationships is that a relationship should remain the same from start to finish. But the woman or man you knew five years ago is not the same today. Each has undergone countless physical, emotional, intellectual, and spiritual changes. With every change, our relationships with these people have changed. Nothing ever remains the same.

When a loved one voices a desire to change—to try new things, to think new thoughts, to live new ways—what do you do? Are you threatened? Do you fear losing the familiar person you've always known? Do you react with criticism or evaluation? Do you ridicule their attempts to experiment with change? Or do you encourage and support their growth?

In order to love another person, we must come to terms with a significant dimension of all relationships—the process of personal growth. We need to understand that change is natural in relationships. We need to accept that our loved ones' dreams might not be our dreams. We need to recognize that we don't always know what is best for another person. We need to acknowledge that we cannot control another person. And most important, we need to realize that one of the most loving things we can do is to encourage our loved ones to grow.

Here are five principles for growing in relationships that you should consider when attempting to encourage growth in a loved one.

Change Is Natural

You're not the same person you were fifteen years ago, ten years ago, or even one year ago. Each day etches its mark on your soul, however slight and imperceptible. Most changes we experience are gradual, such as the physical whispers of advancing age or the inexplicable desire to explore those parts of you that have been long neglected. Other changes are more obvious: the wedding day, the birth of the first child, and the death of a parent. These and hundreds of other life transitions shape the landscape of our lives, marking our growth from the crib to the grave. As you change, so do your loved ones.

How do you encourage your loved ones to explore their own growth and not be threatened by the prospect of change? The first step is to accept the fact that everyone changes. And rather than being a discourager of personal growth and change, be the encourager of your loved ones' dreams. Remember, change is natural.

Their Dreams Are Not Your Dreams

Your loved ones' dreams may not be the ones you would select for yourself, or for them. It wasn't Ron's dream to own a Christmas tree farm. That was Marjorie's dream. Yet Ron accepted how she felt. In Marjorie's words, "He loves me in the way that counts the most—he wants the best for *me*."

In the best relationships I have seen, the people involved recognize that they do not have to be mirror images of each other to be happy. Whether it's romantic partners, family members, or friends, they do not feel the need to have the other person become an exact replica of themselves.

Sure, they can share similar tastes, interests, and goals. Every relationship needs to rest its foundation on some common ground. But in the best relationships, I observe a willingness to appreciate, acknowledge, and encourage the differences as well as the similarities between individuals.

What your loved one desires will not always be what you desire. And that's okay. Life would be very boring if everyone were just like you.

We Don't Know What Is Best for Another Person

As I mentioned earlier, to encourage the growth of our loved ones, we need to accept the fact that their desires might not be your desires. We may be able to do this at the surface level, yet we secretly believe we know what is best for them. Deep down, we may think they're making a mistake by exploring this new idea, interest, or hobby. It's too expensive, they're not cut out for it, or they'll be bored by it, we secretly tell ourselves as we nod our approval.

But we don't really know. We can only guess. At best, we project our likes, interests, and dreams onto them. We tell ourselves, I wouldn't like this activity. But we need to suspend judgment. In fact, we need to do even more than that—we need to wonder with them. Maybe this can be fun. Maybe this is a good idea. Maybe this will turn out all right after all.

In short, we need to stand with them and say, "I'm on your side. If you're interested in this, then so am I." This may be one of the most difficult acts to perform. Yet we owe it to our loved ones to trust their knowledge of what might make them happy. In the end, we must accept the fact that we really don't always know what is best for another person.

We Cannot Control Another Person

Even if you don't want your loved one to pursue a dream or take a class, there isn't much you can do to prevent it in the long run anyway. Sure, you could forbid your loved one to pursue the dream. But ultimately, if the desire is strong enough, you can do little to control another person. It may take five, ten, or twenty years, but if the dream is strong enough, your loved one will find a way to try to breathe life into that dream. Your loved one may even terminate your relationship in order to pursue that dream.

A woman in my relationship class left her husband of twenty-three years because he forbade her to return to college to pursue her dream of becoming a high school English teacher. He owned a successful business and the family was well off financially. Her husband could not understand why she would want to go to school when she already "possessed everything a woman could want." He couldn't understand her desire to teach and didn't make any attempt to listen to her. He simply wouldn't hear of it.

For three years she tried to get her husband's approval to return to college, but to no avail. He would debate with her, bribe her, and even threaten her, but he would never support her desire to become a teacher. Then one day she left the marriage without any warning or ultimatums. Her friends were shocked, and yet not surprised. The woman didn't regret her decision to leave her husband. In fact, she shared with our class that her husband never really encouraged her in any of her interests. She said he only wanted what was best for him.

It may take years, but you will finally discover you can't control another person. Eventually, your loved one will do what she really wants to do, if the desire is great enough. You may be able to bargain, manipulate, shame, or threaten her into compliance for a time, but if her dream is important enough, she may eventually leave you to realize that dream.

Growth Should Be Encouraged

We need to encourage our loved ones to grow—to follow their dreams, to pursue their desires, to fulfill their deepest needs. This act requires that we step aside and let our loved ones take center stage. We need to trust that they ultimately know what is best for themselves. The best feeling in a caring relationship is when your loved ones feel understood and supported, knowing you want what's best for them, not yourself.

Next, we will examine a specific method that can help you support the growth of a loved one.

THE DREAM METHOD TO ENCOURAGE GROWTH

The DREAM Method is a name I give to a series of specific steps you can take to help your loved ones realize their dreams. It not only communicates your desire to be supportive of their dreams and goals, it also assists in the process of helping make those dreams a reality.

DISCUSS the dream.

REFRAIN from evaluation.

EXPERIMENT with the dream.

ACKNOWLEDGE the positives.

MOTIVATE the dreamer.

Step 1: DISCUSS the Dream

In the first step, you provide your loved one with the opportunity to discuss his dream or goal. Your loved one may begin in an informal, unplanned way with a casual remark about wanting to do or accomplish something, or he may make a more formal appeal. The following is a partial dream list to give you an idea of what I mean by a dream and to prepare you for some of the dreams your loved one might present to you:

own a flower shop
change a hairstyle
join a hockey team
learn to play the piano
complete a bachelor's degree
start a business
attend law school
raise llamas
fly an airplane
write a book
attend cosmetology school
teach a sewing class
redecorate the home
act in community theater
volunteer for the fire department
run for city council
own a cabin in the country

As you read this list, you may have cheered some ideas and booed others. Each of these dreams, however, has been someone's strong desire. The more important question is would you be willing to provide the opportunity for your loved one to discuss a dream with you? Or would you meet the dream with criticism, objection, and negative evaluation? If you want to connect with those you love, you should provide the supportive, nonevaluative listening ear they need.

In this first step of the DREAM Method, you let your loved one discuss his dream without interruption, evaluation, or ridicule. Remember your skills in listening and asking open questions? Well, you can put them to work here again!

As your loved one shares the dream with you, ask questions that will encourage him to share, develop, and explore. It doesn't matter if he is considering changing hairstyles or applying to medical school; it's his dream. Here are some questions you might use as you encourage your loved one to discuss his thoughts and opinions:

Tell me more about your dream?
What would this give you?
How long have you had this dream?
What can I do to support your dream?
How can I help you realize your dream?

Not only do you ask your loved one to discuss his ideas and opinions concerning the dream, but you also want to explore his feelings about the dream. The following questions may be helpful:

How do you feel about your dream?
How would you feel after you made this dream come true?
What fears do you have concerning your dream?
How would you feel if I helped you in attaining this dream?

It's also important as your loved one is discussing his dream for you to reflect the feelings you hear being expressed. Here are some feeling questions that can mirror his emotional responses to the discussion:

Are you feeling excited?
You sound like you're feeling apprehensive about all this?
Are you feeling happy about beginning this plan?
Do you feel motivated to pursue this dream?

The most important task you have before you in the first step is to provide a forum for your loved one to discuss his dreams. You are providing him with a safe harbor to explore his thoughts and feelings about the dreams. Be open. Let him explore and play with his dreams. Don't get in the way. You are simply the sounding board for your loved one's ideas.

This first step may require a few minutes. It may take hours. Sometimes it will occur over the course of a few months or even years! It doesn't matter how long it takes. Your only goal is to encourage your loved one to explore a dream.

Step 2: REFRAIN from Evaluation

The second step in the DREAM Method is to refrain from evaluation. This holds true not only for Step 1—discussing the dream—but for all five steps of the process. I realize this may go against your tendency to judge, direct, guide, or control, but this is how you're going to change the old ways you used to communicate. Your main goal is to be on your loved one's side—to give him a chance to dream without getting in the way.

This means more than just refraining from verbally evaluating the discussion. It means refraining from showing dissatisfaction, displeasure, or criticism nonverbally. It means not turning away when he's talking, not messing around with your whittling knife, not frowning, rolling your eyes, smirking, sneering, or laughing. It means being present—really listening with patience, understanding, support, and yes, even a smile or two. Keep in mind that your body communicates your emotions and feelings much more readily than your words, so you need to be supportive with your body as well as your language.

The difficult part of Step 2 is not so much what you don't say and do, but more important, what you think. You may think your loved one's dream is bound to fail because you believe it's unrealistic, flawed, inferior, or just plain stupid and a waste of time. Even though you don't verbally share these thoughts, they may be very apparent by your nonverbal behaviors.

A better way to be supportive is to detach from your negative expectations about your loved one's dream. Let go of being right. Let go of hoping the dream will not be realized. Let go of hoping you'll eventually be able to say "I told you so." Instead, be on your loved one's side for a change. This is one of the most supportive ways to connect with the heart of your loved one.

Step 3: EXPERIMENT with the Dream

In the third step of the process your loved one experiments with the dream by putting some small part of it into action. You do whatever you can to facilitate or assist in the experiment.

Notice I used the word experiment. The person experiments with some small action or behavior to get a feel for pursuing the dream. For example, Marjorie volunteered her Saturdays and then worked part-time to learn the trade rather than immediately purchasing a Christmas tree farm. She experimented by working with trees, getting her hands dirty, and learning the basics of a trade.

The nice thing about experiments is that they're not permanent. Your loved one is just testing the waters. He can always return to the old way of doing things if the experiment doesn't go well. Let me give you a couple of examples of experiments people have attempted.

One eighteen-year-old woman dreamed of writing a book on travel tips for large families. Her father encouraged her to experiment with her dream. Instead of sitting at the typewriter and banging out the first sentence of chapter one, she experimented by typing letters to her friends and relatives. She believed if she could be dedicated enough to write for twenty minutes an evening for a month, she stood a good chance of being dedicated enough to write a 200-page book.

Although she enjoyed writing the letters during the first week, she discovered she quickly lost interest in keeping up her writing schedule after the second week. With her father's support, she decided to modify her experiment by setting a different short-term goal. She would write for twenty minutes, three times a week instead of every night. Instead of writing letters, she would try writing an article for a teen magazine highlighting ten tips for traveling with a large family.

In less than three weeks during this second experiment, she found she lost interest in writing altogether. She discovered she would rather chat with her friends, go to the movies, or read in the recliner than spend her evenings hunched over the typewriter. She slowly realized her dream of writing a book was simply that, a dream. But nothing was really lost. She got to explore a dream. She also realized her dream was something she really didn't want after all, and that's an important discovery.

A second example was a man I counseled who was in his late fifties. He dreamed of getting a bachelor's degree. I met him during his first semester at college. He was enrolled in an art class to see if he could successfully complete a three-unit course. He had never finished high school and his dream was to graduate college. His wife encouraged him to sign up for classes, even though he thought it was a crazy idea at his age. But before he decided to pursue a degree, he wanted to see if he could complete just one class. That was his experiment, a single class.

At an age when most people are retired or at least slowing down, he was beginning a journey usually taken by those decades younger. After his first semester, he discovered that he loved attending college. He completed nine units during the following semester, and within three and one-half years he completed his associate of arts degree in art.

By the time he was sixty-three, he had completed his bachelor of arts degree in art history. Now, at age sixty-six, he is a part-time art teacher in adult education. He accomplished more than he had initially dreamed. And it all started with an experiment—a three-unit art class!

Two people. Two dreams. One wanted to write a book and the other wanted to earn a college degree. They both had three things in common. Each had a dream. Each had the support of a loved one. And each experimented with the dream in a small way before beginning the journey. One decided to pursue a dream and the other did not. But what's important is the fact that each one got the opportunity to explore and experiment with something that was very important—the dream.

Giving loved ones the chance to experiment with a dream without evaluation, ridicule, or punishment is one of the most loving things you'll ever do. Try to be on their side, in their corner when they dream dreams.

When encouraging your loved one to experiment with a dream, keep two things in mind. First, have your loved one experiment with some small aspect of the dream. This is easier, and he's more likely to achieve success. It's easier to write letters than an entire book or to complete one class than finish a degree. Keep the experiment small and manageable.

Second, establish some time limit for experimentation, such as a two-week writing regimen or a one-semester course. This is not to set a limit on the dream. The reason for the time limit is to make the experiment more manageable and feasible for the experimenter. Your purpose is to encourage your loved one to experiment with the dream in a limited but specific way. Then let your loved one decide if the experiment is working or not. It's his dream, not yours.

Step 4: ACKNOWLEDGE the Positives

Once your loved one has begun experimenting with his dream, you should acknowledge the positives of the experiment. Your goal in this phase is to recognize and communicate any positive achievements, accomplishments, results, or victories he has experienced during the experiment. You can accomplish this in two ways. You can verbally compliment any positive results and you can nonverbally show support.

Verbally compliment positive results. Be on the lookout for any positive results during your loved one's experiment. Nothing is too small to notice. This is the real trick—to be able to notice and compliment the small victories and the little achievements that might usually be overlooked, even by the experimenter himself. Don't wait until the final goal or dream is achieved before verbally complimenting his efforts. Begin complimenting early on. This is when acknowledgment and encouragement are most needed.

Remember the woman who wanted to write a book, whose father encouraged her to sit at her typewriter for twenty minutes at a time? The father acknowledged her efforts by lovingly calling her "Anne," in honor of her favorite author, Anne Morrow Lindbergh. She told me he also complimented her on the letters she wrote by remarking how descriptive and humorous they were.

The father didn't wait for his daughter's first book-signing party before he began complimenting. His gift was to compliment and encourage his daughter from the very beginning. The daughter hasn't realized her dream of publishing a book, at least not yet. But she did experience the support and encouragement of her father, who gave the gift of encouraging growth.

The wife of the man whose dream it was to earn a college degree verbally complimented his dedication to simply get up early every Tuesday and Thursday morning to attend his art class. She also recognized and praised his class projects, even when he didn't feel they were worthy of recognition. She didn't wait for her husband to earn his bachelor's degree before beginning her encouragement. She started praising his efforts during his first days of class.

Nonverbally show support. A second way you can acknowledge a positive is to show your support nonverbally. You don't always have to say in words what you can show by behavior or actions. For instance, the father purchased an office lamp and typing paper to support his daughter's efforts to become a writer. And the wife showed her support by making breakfast for her husband on mornings he attended early classes.

Whether it's a banner strung across the driveway proclaiming a minor achievement or a homemade cake with an encouraging message written in chocolate, your nonverbal support and praise will be much appreciated. It really doesn't matter what you do—a bouquet of flowers, a smile, a thoughtful card, a neck massage, or even typing paper—as long as you do something to show your support.

Step 5: MOTIVATE the Dreamer

Every journey, no matter how successful it is ultimately, has its share of difficulties, setbacks, and disappointments. And the dream your loved one will embark on is no exception. He will most likely experience difficulties, disappointments, and failure. That is to be expected. The important point is to motivate your loved one to continue his experiment despite the setbacks.

Each person is responsible for deciding whether or not to continue pursuing a dream. But when your loved one encounters disappointments, minor failures, or disillusionment, you can help motivate by reframing negative results, and highlighting progress.

Reframe negative results. Earlier, we discussed reframing negatives—offering a different interpretation of an event, behavior, or circumstance. Reframing negative events, behaviors, or circumstances can be extremely beneficial in encouraging and motivating an individual who may be disappointed or disillusioned.

Your loved one may have experienced a temporary setback or failure and might complain that the goal or dream will never be realized. Rather than agreeing or saying nothing, you could reframe the event with a positive interpretation. Remember, you don't change the event or circumstance, you simply offer a positive way of interpreting the event or circumstance.

For instance, suppose the man who wanted to earn a college degree received a low score on an exam and he complains that he'll never be able to earn a diploma. That's not the time to agree with his interpretation and suggest he give up.

You could reframe his low score in a positive way by saying, "Another way of looking at this is that it's an invitation to talk with your professor and ask her for some suggestions for studying." Or you could suggest, "This is just one test of many you'll be taking in the future. It's okay if you don't do well on one of them. Even Einstein failed math once."

No matter what disappointment, failure, or difficulty your loved one experiences as he experiments or explores his dream, you can help keep him motivated by seeing the positive in negative events. In the end, it may be your reframing that makes the difference between success and failure.

Highlight progress. Another way to motivate someone who is experiencing disappointment or frustration is to highlight and summarize any progress up to that point. We tend to overlook all our little victories. In discouraging times we need someone to remind us of our achievements. So when your loved one voices disappointment or disillusionment, highlight his progress. To do so requires that you remember his achievements to date. This won't be difficult if you've been acknowledging and complimenting his progress along the way.

GUIDELINES FOR USING THE DREAM METHOD

As you use the DREAM Method to support the growth of a loved one, keep these three guidelines in mind: focus on the journey, not the destination; provide a reality check; and celebrate the decision to discontinue.

Focus on the Journey, Not the Destination

Achieving the dream, regardless of what it is, will be the primary focus of your loved one. Even though the ultimate goal will be broken down into smaller experiments using this method, she will usually have her heart set on achieving the larger dream. During the course of her experiments, remind your loved one to focus on the journey—the process of exploring and experimenting with the various components of the dream.

Remind her to celebrate the little victories along the way: the first few pages of a 200-page book or the B+ received on an art project. Happiness should be experienced and appreciated along the way, not only at the end of the road.

Provide a Reality Check

There could be an occasion when your loved one might entertain a grossly unrealistic, dangerous, or illegal dream or goal. Maybe she dreams of winning the lottery and plans to sell your home and use your life savings to purchase the tickets. Perhaps he wants to grow marijuana in your back-yard to finance a trip to Europe. Or possibly she'd like to trek across the Sahara by herself in hopes of writing an article for *National Geographic*. You need to provide a reality check for your loved one's questionable ambitions.

Before you call the police or the psychiatrist, listen to her explorations of the dream during Steps 1 and 2 of the DREAM Method. Let her discuss the dream and refrain from evaluating while she explores and examines the idea. Do all the things we discussed in Steps 1 and 2, but if you still believe the plan is unrealistic, dangerous, or illegal, confront her with your concerns before she begins experimenting with the dream. Provide a reality check for unrealistic aspirations.

The most important consideration is the physical and emotional well-being of both your loved one and you. If her dream seriously strains the relationship or threatens the health of your loved one, then a reality check might be necessary.

Remember, you should not be accepting a dream that is grossly unrealistic, dangerous, or illegal. You have an ethical obligation to share your concerns and fears regarding unrealistic, unsafe, or illegitimate fantasies.

Celebrate Unrealized Dreams

What if your loved one does not achieve the dream, decides the dream is not worth the effort, or loses interest in the entire affair?

If your loved one does not realize his dream after months or perhaps years of effort, it is not your responsibility to recommend that he abandon his goal. That is his personal decision. In the meantime, be a good listener if he shares his disappointment and frustration with you. Be as supportive, caring, and optimistic as possible. The most significant role you can play is that of the understanding listener. You don't have to rescue or fix the situation. Simply be present and on his side when he shares with you.

If your loved one decides he is no longer interested in pursuing the dream or it's no longer worth the effort, celebrate that decision! Break out the champagne and cake! This is not a time to mourn or regret the effort he has invested. It's a time to celebrate the wonderful experiences he has had during his experimentation with the dream—the skills he acquired, the learning he received, and the new ways he found of perceiving the world and himself.

It's a time to celebrate all the disappointments, frustrations, and failures too! She has learned a great deal about herself through them also. He's gotten a better idea of what he likes and dislikes. All this has come about because they received your support to pursue a dream. They have grown whether or not the dream was realized.

Remind them there are other dreams and other tomorrows. But for now, we will raise our glasses and toast their decision to journey down another road. Cheers.

As you give gifts from your heart, I can think of no better way to support the growth of loved ones than by encouraging them to pursue their dreams. By supporting them in their efforts to explore, you not only provide your loved ones with the encouragement to grow, you give them another way to strengthen the relationship you share. Encourage the dreams and growth of your loved ones. It will change both them and you.

⌒

9.1 **Personal Exploration: What Are Their Dreams?**

For each individual listed below (if applicable), write a brief description of their most important current dream. If you don't know, take a guess. Choose two additional people and describe their dreams.

My mom's dream is _____

My dad's dream is _____

My partner's dream is _____

My son's/daughter's dream is _____

My sister's/brother's dream is _____

My best friend's dream is _____

_____'s dream is _____

_____'s dream is _____

9.2 Practice Giving: Supporting Their Dreams

How did you do with knowing what are the dreams of your loved ones? Were you able to describe your loved ones' dreams?

If so, how might you show your support of their dreams during the next week?

_____

_____

If not, spend some time with your loved ones and discover what their dreams are. How did you feel asking your loved ones about their dreams?

_____

_____

9.3 Practice Giving: Interviewing a Loved One

Share the five steps of the DREAM Method with a loved one and discover how you might be able to support him or her in pursuit of a dream. You might want to do this exercise with all those people you love. Your efforts to show an active interest in their lives and their dreams might change your relationships with them. Be prepared to be surprised.

Name of person you interviewed: _____

How did he or she respond to your interview?

_____

_____

How did you feel about sharing the DREAM Method?

_____

_____

Forgiving Others

∽

"Love is the act of endless forgiveness;
a tender look that becomes a habit."
–Peter Ustinov

Lin smiled easily as she sat in the chair across from me. Her face looked far younger than her twenty-two years, and it masked the resentment she held toward her father. Living at home with her dad, mom, and two younger brothers was becoming intolerable for Lin. Vietnamese refugees, her family immigrated to America when she was thirteen, and learning the ways of this new country was not easy, especially for her father.

Over the past nine years, her dad had increasingly accused Lin of becoming "too American." He didn't approve of her clothes, her music, or her white friends. She gradually discovered that her conflict and anger toward her father were becoming unbearable. She wanted to move out on her own, but she couldn't afford to as a part-time college student. This issue brought her into therapy.

During her fourth counseling session, I asked about the homework I had assigned the previous week. Her task was to apologize to her father for being disrespectful during a recent argument and to ask for his forgiveness. When I initially suggested this assignment, Lin was reluctant to even consider apologizing because she felt justified in her anger toward her dad. But after explaining that holding on to anger affects her much more than it affects her father, she decided to give it a try.

"I did what you told me to do," Lin began.

"How did that feel, asking for forgiveness?" I inquired.

"It wasn't easy, because my dad is not a talker. To make things worse, he didn't say anything right after I asked him to forgive me. He just walked out of the room looking mad."

"I'm not concerned about his response," I interrupted. "You have no control over your father's response, whether he accepts, rejects, or walks out. All you can do is forgive him and ask for his forgiveness. That is the only thing you have control over—your decision to forgive."

"Well, it's funny," continued Lin. "Since Tuesday night, that's when I did it, he's been a lot nicer to me. Maybe he's changing. I hope so."

"Maybe you're changing," I added.

"Maybe," she smiled.

We will all be hurt by those we love and we will also hurt others. In any relationship we will suffer disappointment, frustration, and pain. The hurts you experience will most likely be minor—an unfair criticism, a broken promise, or a bit of gossip. A few may be more serious. But you will experience hurt in any relationship. We have little control over that. However, we can control what we do with our hurt. We can let go of the hurt and guilt and decide to give the gift of forgiving others.

Forgiveness is the act of granting free pardon for an offense. In essence, it is letting go of the desire to get even, to make people pay for the hurt they may have caused you. It is the act of letting someone off the hook for hurting you. To grant free pardon means you voluntarily pardon or excuse the individual who hurt you, at no cost to them. There is nothing the person has to do, no price he has to pay, for you to excuse him for his offense. Forgiveness, however, goes against our very nature.

Our natural inclination is to get even, to retaliate, to punish those who cause us pain. Many of us have been coached to "even the score," " make them pay," and take "an eye for an eye." But the act of retaliation, if successful, is hollow indeed. Very few of us feel better after we've made a victim of our victimizer. And rarely do we feel like celebrating after we have brought equivalent suffering to those who have made us suffer. Getting even only makes us feel more guilt. Retaliation bears even a higher price than victimization.

What you do with this anger will determine to a large extent the kind of person you will become and the quality of all your relationships. If you choose to hold on to hurt and anger, you will become bitter. And this bitterness will infiltrate every area of your relationships. It may not always be observable, but it will affect all your relationships to some degree.

So, what is the answer? Forgiveness. Forgiveness might be the single most difficult communication gift you will be asked to give in this book. But it may also be the most liberating gift. In Lin's case, by asking her father for forgiveness, she was also forgiving him—and letting go of some of the hurt and anger she held.

TYPES OF FORGIVENESS

We will explore two specific instances of forgiving others. The first instance is when the person apologizes and asks your forgiveness and the second instance is when the person is not apologetic. No matter which of the two responses the other individual chooses, your goal is to forgive him or her.

Forgiving Those Who Ask for Your Forgiveness

If someone who has wronged you asks for your forgiveness, you need to seriously consider forgiving him. Instances of repeated or chronic physical or emotional abuse do not warrant the same consideration as less dangerous offenses, but you need to consider the violation, the person's sincerity, and the probability of recurrence.

Forgiveness is not a feeling, but a decision. You need to forgive people if you are to be free. If you decide not to forgive, you, not the other person, may carry the weight of anger and resentment. Forgive those who ask for forgiveness, if it's at all possible.

Forgiving Those Who Are Not Apologetic

There will be occasions when someone hurts you and is not apologetic, let alone repentant enough to ask you for forgiveness. In this instance, you must forgive the person anyway.

You may not want to forgive her initially. In fact, you may never feel the desire to forgive her for the wrong she has done you. But remember, forgiveness is not a feeling, it's your decision to be free of hurt and anger.

You will probably never feel like forgiving them. However, you can make the conscious decision to let go of your pain. It's for yourself that you decide to forgive. Forgiving those who have hurt you, even if they are not repentant, is the only way you will move beyond the anger you feel.

WAYS TO FORGIVE

There are four ways you can forgive those who have hurt you and refuse to be apologetic. You can pretend to forgive, imagine their death, ask for their forgiveness, and forgive them directly.

Pretend to Forgive

The first method I refer to as pretending to forgive. It can be used when the hurt is too recent or too serious for you to even consider forgiving the other person. Pretending to forgive the other person gives you a chance to feel something other than anger, vengeance, or self-pity.

Here's how the method works. Place two chairs about three feet apart, facing each another. Sit in one of the chairs and imagine the person who hurt you in the empty chair. Next, pretend you have decided to forgive this person (even though you have not really made this decision). In fact, "tell" the other person you have forgiven him. Picture the person's face softening as you forgive him. Imagine the other person saying something thoughtful, considerate, or even apologetic. After you have forgiven the person, just sit in your chair and feel your response to the exercise. Do you feel the same? Do you feel a slight change? Do you still feel the hurt or anger?

This entire process of "pretending to forgive" will take a minute or two at most. I have been surprised by the changes in my heart when I pretend to forgive someone, even when I still haven't decided to forgive the person. By pretending to forgive, often my anger, vengeance, or self-pity becomes less potent. It frees me to consider other ways of dealing with my hurt or anger.

Imagine Their Death

The second method of dealing with those who are not apologetic is called imagining their death. This method can soften your attitude toward the other person. It involves imagining the person has only one day to live.

Sit quietly and explore what this would mean to you if the person who hurt you would die in the next twenty-four hours. Do you feel the same? Do you feel slightly different? Do you still focus on yourself and your hurt? Or are you thinking about the other person? Have your feelings changed about the relative importance of the offense compared with the person's impending death?

My experience with this exercise is one of freedom. When I imagine no longer being able to see this individual, I am no longer as concerned about getting even, punishing, or changing the individual. I usually feel liberated from the person. It's strange, but this technique helps me feel more compassionate, understanding, and loving toward that person.

Ask for Their Forgiveness

The third method I refer to as asking for their forgiveness. This is not an exercise, but rather an actual activity you perform. I don't tell individuals that I forgive them for what they did; instead I ask them *to forgive me*. I ask them to forgive me for the negative feelings (anger, vengeance, resentment, bitterness, and so forth) I might have held against them.

Asking their forgiveness is powerful and often brings about startling results. I remember a colleague I worked with some years ago who hurt my feelings by some unfair remarks he had made about me to a number of mutual acquaintances. I learned of these remarks from two people. I was hurt by his criticisms and I harbored resentment and anger toward him.

After three weeks of being nice to his face, yet holding onto these feelings of anger, I decided to do something about it. I walked into his office one morning and asked if he had a few minutes to talk. He politely agreed, and I proceeded to explain to him that I had heard about some remarks he allegedly had made about me. I didn't say what the remarks were or whether it was true that he made them. I told him what had been bothering me were the ugly feelings I had been harboring against him and how these feelings were actually hurting me. I told him I was wrong not to bring this issue to his attention earlier. I was wrong to harbor these feelings against him for so long. I apologized for doing so and asked him to forgive me. The entire event took less than forty-five seconds.

My colleague looked stunned. He denied saying most of the things I mentioned and briefly defended those things he did admit. I quickly intervened and said I wasn't interested in what he said or didn't say. What

I was interested in was apologizing for the bad feelings I held against him and to ask for his forgiveness. He took a deep breath, then replied, "Of course." I walked out of his office and experienced the freedom that accompanies forgiveness.

I'm glad I did, because less than eight weeks later my colleague died of a heart attack. We had worked in the same department for nineteen years and had shared the normal ups and downs experienced in any relationship. To this day I'm thankful I chose to talk with him. Had I not, I would have undoubtedly felt regret.

Forgive Them Directly

The final method for forgiving others is forgiving them directly. After you have decided to forgive other people for their offense, you share your decision with them in person, face-to-face. The primary weakness of this method is that people often respond with denial, justification, rationalization, or blame. They might deny that they did in fact offend you. They could try to justify their words or behavior. They may rationalize what they did as for your own good. Or they might blame you for the entire incident, claiming complete innocence.

No matter what response they choose, emphasize the fact that you have chosen to forgive them for their offense. Remind them you are not there to debate, explore, or analyze the issue. You are simply there to tell them you have forgiven them of the offense and you hold nothing against them. You don't have to be best friends after the meeting. The purpose for the meeting is to let them know you have forgiven them. Plain and simple.

Now that we've explored four ways to forgive others, we direct our attention to the process of asking others for their forgiveness.

ASKING FOR FORGIVENESS

If you have wronged a loved one and want to ask for forgiveness, try the AAA Forgiveness Method:

A D M I T you were wrong.

A P O L O G I Z E for the offense.

A S K their forgiveness.

Let's assume you criticized your loved one in front of friends at a party. There was a brief argument over the incident on the way home, but you defended your actions. The incident was never mentioned again. Yet in the next few days you begin to feel guilty about your behavior. You decide to ask for forgiveness. Here's how the AAA Forgiveness Method works:

You: Honey, do you remember the party last Saturday night?

Honey: I've been trying to forget.

You: Well, **I was wrong** to criticize you in front of your friends. (admitting your were wrong)

Honey: You bet you were. That was a terrible thing to do. Would I ever do something like that to you?

You: No. Probably not. But **I apologize** for criticizing you. **I'm sorry.** (apologizing for the offense)

Honey: Apology accepted, I guess.

You: **Would you forgive me** for criticizing you? (asking for forgiveness)

Honey: Well, yes. Of course I'll forgive you.

Not all attempts at asking for forgiveness will go this smoothly, but I wanted you to see how the AAA Forgiveness Method might work under cooperative circumstances.

Did you notice how the first two steps involved declarative statements? You admit you were wrong (a statement). And you apologize for the offense (a statement). But the third step asks a question—asking for forgiveness. After you ask, the ball is in the other person's court and he must decide what to do with your request. You no longer have a decision to make because you have already decided to ask him to forgive you. Your job is complete. He must decide to forgive you or not.

If he forgives you—great! That's what we're hoping he'll do. If he doesn't forgive you—that's okay! You can walk away from the exchange knowing you did the right thing. Knowing you admitted you were wrong, apologized for the offense, and asked for forgiveness. There's nothing more you could have done. And now you're free, no matter what he decides to do with the question you presented.

The most important thing is that you decided to change your position about your offense. Instead of denying, justifying, rationalizing, blaming, or projecting your offense, you chose to take responsibility for it. And by taking responsibility and asking forgiveness, you altered the balance of your relationship with that person. Instead of hiding, you have come out into the open. Instead of being hard, you have chosen to be soft. The relationship is no longer the same. Your decision to ask for forgiveness has changed the relationship. You were mature enough to admit you were wrong and apologize for your offense. But most important, you asked for forgiveness.

Rehearse Your Request

If you plan to ask someone for forgiveness, you may want to rehearse the AAA Forgiveness Method once or twice beforehand. I find it helpful to sit, face an empty chair, and hold a practice run. Just pretend the other person is sitting in the empty chair and make your three statements.

Don't try to second-guess what the other person will say or do. Simply trust that all will go smoothly and you will be heard. Make your statements brief and speak in a slow and gentle voice. Don't rush the words. Don't force a favorable response. Just state your words gently and confidently. Remember that once you have asked people for forgiveness, the decision to forgive is theirs, not yours.

GUIDELINES FOR FORGIVENESS

To forgive and to ask for forgiveness requires you to abandon your usual, familiar way of dealing with hurt, anger, and guilt. Here are four guidelines to keep in mind about forgiveness—forgiveness is a decision, not a feeling; forgiveness requires suspension of your ego; some people will not forgive; and forgiveness is a never-ending process.

Forgiveness Is a Decision, Not a Feeling

Two erroneous concepts about forgiveness are that you should feel the need to ask for forgiveness before you make the request and that you should feel like forgiving someone before you communicate your forgiveness.

Forgiveness is a decision to consciously let go of your guilt or anger. Initially, forgiveness has more to do with your head than your heart. If you waited until you felt like asking for forgiveness or granting forgiveness, you'd wait forever. Very few of us are so magnanimous or understanding that we would undertake forgiveness on our feelings alone. Our natural inclination is to take revenge on those who have hurt us or to justify the hurt we have caused others.

Don't use the excuse that you don't feel like asking for forgiveness or you don't feel you want to forgive someone for an offense. Forgiveness is not a feeling; it's a decision. Your decision not to forgive or ask for forgiveness will keep you imprisoned by anger and guilt. It will limit the depth of your relationships with others, and with yourself, and eventually it will be you who pays the highest price for holding on to feelings of anger or guilt. You must ultimately decide to let go in order to be free.

Forgiveness Requires Suspension of the Ego

Your decision to forgive or ask for forgiveness is difficult. The act of forgiveness demands the suspension of your ego. You will have to put yourself second for a while—not all the time or forever, but occasionally. In order to be in relationships, we must develop our ability to put others first, and ourselves second. It's the process of stepping aside and allowing our loved ones to take center stage. It is not easy to occasionally suspend preoccupation with ourselves. Yet it is essential in our journey to the hearts of others.

To make connections with others, we must suspend our ego for a time, to let the other person have the limelight. We need to set aside preoccupation with our ideas, attitudes, beliefs, and feelings, and be open to the reality of another person. If we do not suspend our ego, we will never be fully free to ask for forgiveness or to grant forgiveness to others because we will always be focused on our feelings of anger or guilt. Instead, let go of bad feelings by giving the gift of forgiveness. Step aside long enough to let in your loved ones.

Some People Will Not Forgive You

You need to remember that when you request forgiveness some people will not forgive you. And you must somehow learn to accept this fact, or else be disappointed, hurt, or angry. As I said earlier, it's not necessary that the person forgives you. What's most important is that you decided to change your position regarding your offense. You chose to accept responsibility for your actions. By asking for forgiveness, you abandoned your position to be right or justified in your actions. Instead, you elected to reestablish those connections with a loved one.

Forgiveness Is a Never-Ending Process

Whether we have made the decision to ask for forgiveness or grant forgiveness, the process of forgiving is ongoing. Often in therapy, a client will forgive someone for an offense, but the old feelings of hurt and anger will resurface later. The client will feel frustrated and depressed by his failure to be fully rid of these uncomfortable feelings. He will frequently complain about the return of the anger or hurt.

But the resurfacing of these feelings is natural and should not be avoided. In fact, it is to be expected. There is no magical cure for pain and suffering. The process of forgiving is not a quick and easy remedy for the anger and guilt we experience. It may require months, perhaps years, to recover fully from a hurt. In some instances, maybe we never recover fully from some of life's most painful sufferings.

Forgiving is not a destination. Rather, forgiving is a way of traveling. It is actually something we become over time—a forgiving individual. Forgiving demands of us the greatest of all tasks—the willingness to permit others, and ourselves, to make mistakes, to break promises, and to never fully measure up. If we were truly perfect, we would never be called on to forgive. But we are human and will always fall short of the mark. If you want to be in loving relationships with other people, you will find it necessary to give the gift of forgiving others.

꙼

10.1 Personal Exploration: Recalling Past Hurts

Recall a past hurt with a loved one. Think about your initial feelings and what you did with your feelings.

Are you satisfied with what you did? _____

What would you do differently if the event happened again?

_____

_____

_____

What are your responses to this exercise?

_____

_____

_____

_____

10.2 Practice Giving: Forgiveness Role-Play

Have a friend or loved one role-play someone from whom you need to ask forgiveness. Give your role-play partner details on how to speak and behave like the individual they are playing. Whenever your partner is ready, go through the three steps of the AAA Forgiveness Method.

How did this role-play feel?

_____

_____

_____

Will you try to actually ask forgiveness from the person? Why or why not?

_____

_____

_____

What are your responses to this exercise?

_____

_____

_____

_____

10.3 Practice Giving: Forgiving Yourself

Undoubtedly you feel guilty about some thoughts, actions, or behaviors for which you haven't yet forgiven yourself. Try giving the gift of forgiveness to yourself.

About what thought, action, or behavior do you still feel guilty?

_____

_____

Write yourself a brief one-paragraph letter offering forgiveness for what you did.

What are your responses to this letter?

_____

_____

_____

_____

Afterword

～

"Knowledge is useless
until it is put into practice."
–John F. Kennedy

The knock at the door came as I was getting ready to leave my office for the day. I welcomed the visitor and offered him a chair. He was a former student from my relationship class and he shook my hand enthusiastically and smiled cheerfully. I didn't recall Reggie ever being particularly enthusiastic or cheerful. Most of the semester he appeared reluctant, almost antagonistic toward me and the activities I required of the students in the relationship course. Frankly, I was surprised by his visit.

"I just had to stop by and say thanks for last semester," he began.

"You're welcome. How's it been going, Reggie?" I asked.

"Really good. You know all those gifts you had us do in class? Well, I really didn't do them all. I made up some of my homework reports," he admitted.

"Oh, really?"

"Yeah. I couldn't get into the class much. It just seemed too lame. But I stuck it out because my mom forced me to. But something happened this past semester. I saw my dad when he came to California for a visit. He and my mom have been divorced since I was two, and I've only seen him a couple of times," Reggie confided.

"I didn't know this."

"Yeah. Anyway," he continued, "he took me out to lunch and we talked. During our lunch, I told him I was sorry for hating him all my life. I told him a lot of the bad stuff I felt toward him since I was a kid. And then I asked him to forgive me for carrying so much hatred for him—just like we practiced in class."

"You asked your dad to forgive you?" I asked, surprised by his words.

143
～

"My dad just cried, right there in the restaurant. It blew my mind. We hugged and talked some more. It was great! Well, anyway, he asked me to visit him in Chicago this summer and I'm going. I just wanted you to know. Thanks."

To receive love, we must become love. The gifts you give from your heart will improve, strengthen, and, in Reggie's case, reestablish the love relationships that are important to you. Love is really about giving and not receiving. Love requires that we move from self-centeredness to other-centeredness in our journey called life.

This book showed you ten gifts you can give from your heart that will connect you to those you love. But these gifts will be useless until you decide to give them away. Love requires that you take a risk and give at least one gift from the heart, as Reggie did. And his decision could mark the beginning of a loving relationship that will last his entire lifetime.

Knowledge of these gifts is useless until they are put into practice. It is my hope that you will accept this invitation and decide to give gifts from your heart.

Bibliography

Introduction. Relationships Require Giving

Bach, G. *Pairing*. New York: William Morrow, 1972.

Gibran, Kahlil. *The Prophet*. New York: Alfred A. Knopf, 1983.

Grant, Gwendolyn. *The Best Kind of Loving*. New York: HarperPerennial, 1995.

Hanh, Thich Nhat. *Every Step Is Peace*. New York: Bantam Books, 1991.

Merton, Thomas. *New Seeds of Contemplation*. New York: New Directions, 1991.

Moore, Thomas. *Care of the Soul*. New York: HarperCollins, 1992.

Nouwen, Henri. *Reaching Out*. New York: Doubleday, 1966.

Viorst, Judith. *Necessary Losses*. New York: Simon & Schuster, 1986.

Gift 1. Deciding to Give

Dass, Ram. *How Can I Help?* New York: Alfred A. Knopf, 1985.

Fromm, Erich. *The Art of Loving*. New York: Harper & Brothers, 1956.

Haley, Jay. *Uncommon Therapy*. New York: Norton, 1988.

Kingma, Daphne. *Finding True Love*. Berkeley, Calif.: Conary Press, 1996.

Rubin, Lillian. *Intimate Strangers*. New York: Harper & Row, 1983.

Williamson, Marianne. *A Return to Love*. New York: HarperCollins, 1992.

Wilmot, W. *Dyadic Communication*. New York: Random House, 1987.

Gift 2. Communicating for Connection

Adler, M. *How to Speak, How to Listen*. New York: Macmillan, 1983.

Allen, Patricia. *Staying Married and Loving It*. New York: William Morrow, 1997.

Condon, John. *Semantics and Communication*. New York: Macmillan, 1985.

Ellis, D. G. *From Language to Communication*. Hillsdale, N. J.: Lawrence Erlbaum, 1992.

Jourard, S. *The Transparent Self*. New York: Litton, 1971.

Jung, Carl. *Man and His Symbols*. New York: Doubleday, 1991.

Lao-tzu. *Tao Te Ching*. New York: Random House, 1972.

Littlejohn, S. W. *Theories of Human Communication*. Belmont, Calif.: Wadsworth, 1989.

Peck, M. Scott. *The Road Less Traveled*. New York: Touchstone, 1978.

Pennebaker, J. *Opening Up: The Healing Power of Confiding in Others*. New York: Avon, 1990.

Powell, John. *The Secret of Staying in Love*. New York: Argus, 1994.

Tannen, Deborah. *You Just Don't Understand*. New York: Ballantine, 1990.

Gift 3. Accepting Others

Andrews, Lynn. *Love and Power*. New York: HarperCollins, 1997.

Beattie, Melody. *Journey to the Heart*. San Francisco: Harper, 1996.

Buber, Martin. *I-Thou*. New York: Charles Scribner's Sons, 1970.

Buscaglia, Leo. *Living, Loving, and Learning*. New York: Ballantine, 1982.

Gaber, A. *How to Talk So Kids Will Listen & Listen So Kids Will Talk*. New York: Avon, 1982.

Jung, C. G. *The Undiscovered Self*. New Jersey: Princeton University Press, 1990.

Rogers, Carl. *On Becoming a Person*. Boston: Houghton Mifflin, 1972.

Stewart, John. *Together; Communicating Interpersonally*. New York: McGraw-Hill, 1980.

Gift 4. Listening for Understanding

Adler, Ron. *Looking Out, Looking In*. New York: Harcourt Brace, 1996.

Axline, Virginia. *Dibs: In Search of Self*. New York: Ballantine Books, 1992.

Blanchard, Margaret. *From the Listening Place*. Portland, Maine: Astarte Shell Press, 1997.

Brownell, J. *Building Active Listening Skills*. Englewood Cliffs, N.J.: Prentice-Hall, 1986.

Burley-Allen, Madelyn. *Listening, the Forgotten Skill*. New York; John Wiley & Sons, 1996.

Caroll, John B. *Language, Thought, and Reality: Selected Writings of Lee Whorf, 5/e*. Cambridge, Mass.: MIT Press, 1970.

Gordon, Thomas. *Parent Effectiveness Training*. New York: Wyden, 1970.

Peck, M. Scott. *The Road Less Traveled*. New York: Touchstone, 1978.

Rogers, Carl. *Client-Centered Therapy*. Boston: Houghton Mifflin, 1951.

Steil, Lyman. *Effective Listening*. New York: Addison-Wesley, 1983.

Wolvin, Andrew. *Listening*. Madison, Wis.: Brown Benchmark, 1996.

Gift 5. Asking Questions

Adler, Ron. *Looking Out, Looking In.* New York: Harcourt Brace, 1996.

Beebe, S. *Family Talk.* New York: Random House, 1986.

Boulton, R. *People Skills.* New York: Simon & Schuster, 1979.

Erickson, Milton. *Hypnotic Therapies.* New York: Irvington, 1976.

Gordon, Sol. *Is There Anything I Can Do?* New York: Dell, 1994.

Watzlawick, Paul. *Language of Change.* New York: Basic Books, 1987.

Gift 6. Enlarging Others

Carnegie, Dale. *How to Win Friends and Influence People.* New York: Spire, 1982.

Garner, Alan. *Conversationally Speaking.* New York: McGraw Hill, 1980.

Gattuso, Joan. *A Course in Love.* San Francisco: Harper, 1996.

Hendrick, C. *Romantic Love.* Newbury Park, Calif.: Sage, 1991.

McGinnis, Leroy. *The Friendship Factor.* New York: Argus, 1991.

Gift 7. Flowing with Conflict

Fisher, R. *Getting to Yes.* New York: Viking Press, 1991.

Fujishin, Randy. *Discovering the Leader Within.* San Francisco: Acada Books, 1997.

Hocker, J. *Interpersonal Conflict.* Dubuque, Iowa: Brown, 1985.

Kopp, S. *Back to One.* Palo Alto, Calif.: Science and Behavior Books, 1977.

Robbin-Jones, Riki. *Negotiating Love.* New York: Ballantine, 1995.

Satir, V. *Making Contact.* Millbrae, Calif.: Celestial Arts Press, 1976.

Stewart, J. *Bridges, Not Walls.* New York: McGraw-Hill, 1995.

Gift 8. Showing You Care

Burgoon, J. K. *Nonverbal Communication.* New York: HarperCollins, 1989.

Cane, William. *The Art of Hugging.* New York: St. Martins Griffen, 1996.

Colton, Helen. *Touch Therapy.* New York: Zebra Books, 1983.

Hall, Edward. *The Silent Language.* New York: Ballantine, 1990.

Knapp, M. L. *Nonverbal Communication and Human Interaction.* New York: Holt, Rinehart & Winston, 1992.

Kottler, Jeffrey. *The Language of Tears.* San Francisco, Jossey-Bass, 1996.

Leathers, D. G. *Successful Nonverbal Communication.* New York: Macmillan, 1992.

Montagu, Ashley. *Touching.* New York: Harper & Row, 1986.

Gift 9. Encouraging Growth

Breathnach, Sarah. *Simple Abundance.* New York: Warner, 1995.

Gallagher, Winnifred. *Just the Way You Are.* New York: Random House, 1996.

Gordon, Arthur. *A Touch of Wonder.* Old Tappan, N.J.: Spire Books, 1990.

Jung, Carl. *Analytic Psychology.* New York: Vintage Books, 1968.

Lindbergh, Anne Morrow. *Gift from the Sea.* New York: Pantheon, 1992.

Suzuki, Shunryu. *Zen Mind, Beginner's Mind.* New York: Weatherhill, 1990.

Gift 10. Forgiving Others

Church, Forrest. *Life Lines.* Boston: Beacon Press, 1996.

Hay, Louise. *You Can Heal Your Life.* Carlsbad, Calif.: Hay House, 1984.

Klein, Charles. *How to Forgive When You Can't Forget.* New York: Berkeley Books, 1997.

Kübler-Ross, Elisabeth. *On Death and Dying.* London: Macmillan, 1969.

Prather, H. *Notes to Myself.* Moab, Utah: Real People Press, 1970.

Simon, Sidney. *Forgiveness.* New York: Time Warner, 1990.

Smedes, Lewis. *Forgive and Forget.* San Francisco: Harper, 1996.

Index